Prophets for Our Time

An Exposition of Obadiah and Jonah

JARL K. WAGGONER

RESOURCE *Publications* • Eugene, Oregon

PROPHETS FOR OUR TIME
An Exposition of Obadiah and Jonah

Resource Publications
An Imprint of Wipf and Stock Publishers
199 W. 8th Ave., Suite 3
Eugene, OR 97401

www.wipfandstock.com

ISBN 13: 978-1-60608-957-6

Manufactured in the U.S.A.

To my parents
Sam and Evelyn Waggoner,
with deepest appreciation
for their encouragement, support, and example

Prophets for Our Time

Contents

Acknowledgments

JOHN DONNE SAID THAT no man is an island. Any honest author feels the same way about his writing. It is never his work alone. It is the product of study, informed by the study of others. It is the product of the author's own experiences and that of others. It is the product of his parents, teachers, spouse, friends, and perhaps even enemies. It is the product of his education and life philosophy. And it is a creative product that in the end should give honor to the author of creativity.

This author must humbly acknowledge the contributions of at least a few of those who contributed to the completion of this work. They are all to be credited in some degree with whatever value it achieves and whatever glory accrues to the Lord Jesus Christ.

Evelyn Waggoner, my mother, transcribed by hand some of the sermons that formed the basis for this series of studies. It was a labor of love that is greatly appreciated.

My wife Winona was a very able proofreader and offered a number of helpful suggestions that made this work far better than it otherwise would have been.

My friend James Coffey offered some valuable suggestions for which I am most grateful, and my oldest son, Jarrell, provided some much needed help with formatting.

The congregation of Cornerstone Bible Church in Lancaster, South Carolina offered me great encouragement simply by listening and responding to my messages from Obadiah and Jonah.

Thanks also to my children, Jarrell, Austin, Reed, Logan, and Kalissa, who provided motivation and an atmosphere that allowed me to complete a work that was as much for them as for anyone else.

Abbreviations

BDB—A Hebrew and English Lexicon of the Old Testament, ed. Francis Brown, S. R. Driver, and Charles A. Briggs (Reprint, Oxford: Clarendon Press, 1978).

NASB —New American Standard Bible

NIV—New International Version

NKJV—New King James Version

NJB—New Jerusalem Bible

KJV—King James Version

NRSV—New Revised Standard Version

TWOT—Theological Wordbook of the Old Testament, ed. R. Laird Harris, Gleason L. Archer, and Bruce K. Waltke, 2 vols. (Chicago: Moody Press, 1980).

Note: Transliterations of Hebrew characters follow that used in *TWOT.*

Preface

THE BOOKS OF OBADIAH and Jonah might not seem to be particularly important in the great scheme of Scripture. Neatly tucked away among the so-called Minor Prophets of the Old Testament and written some 2800 years ago, they can be read in just ten minutes. These two brief prophetic books, however, contain valuable lessons for people of the twenty-first century.

The story of Jonah is somewhat familiar to most people—at least they recall the amusing story of the prophet who was swallowed by a fish—but the book itself is seldom appreciated for its rich but often uncomfortable lessons for people today. While there is some familiarity with Jonah, the same usually cannot be said for the book of Obadiah. Even to most Christians Obadiah remains an obscure little book with an equally obscure message directed toward a nation that can no longer be found on our maps.

On the surface the two books seem to have little in common, apart from the fact that they stand side by side in our Bibles and were written within a hundred years of one another. One is a prophecy, written in that strange prophetic language of the Old Testament; the other is a narrative account of Jonah's experiences. Obadiah reveals almost nothing about the prophet who wrote the book; Jonah reveals much of the author's thoughts and attitudes. Obadiah speaks to Edom, a nation immediately south of the Holy Land and inhabited by a Semitic people; Jonah deals with the Assyrian people of Nineveh, far to the north and east of Israel.

As different as they might appear, however, these two prophetic books address common themes—pride, selfishness, self-sufficiency, obedience, violence, vengeance, and grace. As such, it is quite proper to study these books together.

God's inspired, inerrant Word is always worthy of our study, regardless of the issues any portion of it might address. But the matters we encounter in the books of Obadiah and Jonah are especially relevant, for they entail attitudes and actions we struggle with in our personal lives almost on a daily basis. These books, therefore, can quite properly be called prophets for our time.

These studies were originally presented in the form of sermons delivered at Cornerstone Bible Church in Lancaster, South Carolina. Many of the illustrations have been retained, along with the emphasis on practical and personal application. The studies therefore are designed not to be used primarily as a reference but to be *read*. They can even be read devotionally, but they also should be read thoughtfully. These are not just a series of devotional thoughts on the text of Obadiah and Jonah but an attempt to explain the meaning of the text so that there is proper understanding and application of it. I have tried to avoid too much technical detail, while at the same time dealing adequately with the details of the underlying Hebrew text. The footnotes will direct interested readers to the sources supporting my conclusions.

The Bible is God's infallible revelation to mankind. Yet fallible human beings do not always find it easy to grasp the mind of the God whose ways are higher than our ways (Isa. 55:9). This work is by no means an infallible interpretation of the prophets' writings, but it is my hope and prayer that by the grace of God and the illuminating work of God the Holy Spirit it will give the reader a greater understanding of our God and his ways.

Jarl K. Waggoner

Exposition
of
Obadiah

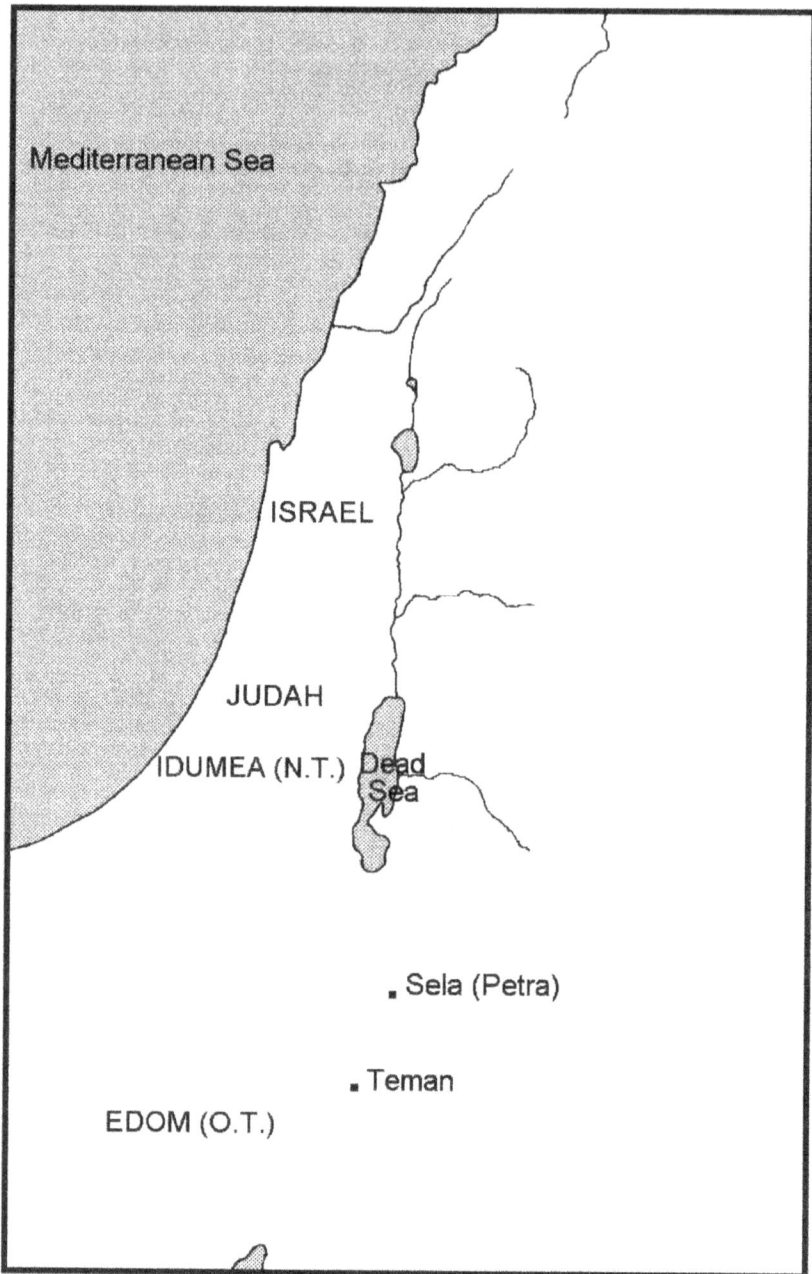

Mediterranean Sea

ISRAEL

JUDAH

IDUMEA (N.T.)

Dead
Sea

. Sela (Petra)

. Teman

EDOM (O.T.)

1

Introduction to Obadiah

W E AMERICANS HAVE AN interesting expression to describe what
happens when a person receives an especially effective and well-
deserved reprimand. We say that person has been "put in his place." When
someone steps over the line of propriety or etiquette, we are elated—at
least inwardly—to see that person put in his or her place. The ancient
nation of Edom had forgotten its place in God's plan. Essentially, the book
of Obadiah is about God putting Edom in its place.

Obadiah begins with these words:

> The vision of Obadiah. Thus says the Lord God concerning Edom–
> We have heard a report from the Lord,
> And an envoy has been sent among the nations saying,
> "Arise and let us go against her for battle"—
> Behold, I will make you small among the nations;
> You are greatly despised.

It immediately becomes apparent from these first two verses of
Obadiah that the book is a pronouncement of judgment upon the nation
of Edom. As we consider these two verses, some questions naturally come
to mind: What do we know about Edom, and why does God take this
entire book—short though it is—to declare his judgment on this nation?
What had the Edomites done to deserve this kind of judgment?

THE ORIGIN OF EDOM

In order to understand the book of Obadiah, we need to glance briefly
at the history of the nation of Edom. That history begins in the book of
Genesis. Genesis 36:1 says, "Now these are the records of the generations
of Esau (that is, Edom)." Edom was simply another name for Esau, the

son of Isaac. Esau had earned the name "Edom," which means "red,"[1] back in Genesis 25. There he had traded his birthright to his brother Jacob for some red food (vv. 29–34). In Genesis 36 we are reminded that Edom was another name for Esau. In verses 8 and 9 we are told, "So Esau lived in the hill country of Seir; Esau is Edom. These then are the records of the generations of Esau the father of the Edomites in the hill country of Seir." Esau thus was the progenitor of the people known as Edomites.

From the very beginning of the Edomite nation in the person of Esau, the destiny of that nation was set forth in prophecy. When Rebekah, the wife of Isaac, was about to bear twins, the children "struggled together within her" (Gen. 25:22). Some unusual movement in the womb caused her to enquire of the Lord what was happening to her, and in some way the Lord answered her, saying, "Two nations are in your womb; and two peoples shall be separated from your body; and one people shall be stronger than the other; and the older shall serve the younger" (v. 23). Thus, even before Esau was born, it was determined that he, the older of the twin sons, would serve his younger brother Jacob. Furthermore, the Lord declared that this subservience would be realized in the people and nations that would come forth from these two brothers. Edom, the descendants of Esau, would serve Israel, the descendants of Jacob.

The struggle between the two brothers first appears when Jacob used the "red stew" to extort the birthright from his older brother.[2] It reappears in Genesis 27. We must realize, of course, that much deception was going on here. In fact, when Isaac pronounced his blessing upon Jacob, he thought he was speaking the words to Esau. This whole episode does not speak highly of the characters of any of the players—Isaac, Jacob, Esau, or Rebekah. Still, the sovereign Lord was using even the wicked ways of human beings to bring about his eternal purposes. The Lord was not going to let Isaac's blessing—which Isaac intended for Esau—contradict what he already had declared prophetically to Rebekah in Genesis 25:23.

---

1. The name "Esau" means "hairy." The name "Edom," which means "red," also fits Esau, not only because of the incident with the meat but also because of his red appearance at birth. See H. C. Leupold, *Exposition of Genesis* (Grand Rapids: Baker, 1942), 2:711.

2. By custom the birthright belonged to the oldest son. With it came a double portion of the father's inheritance and precedence over the other children, even while his father lived. Apparently, the birthright was formalized by the father's spoken blessing and under certain circumstances could be transferred to another son. See John J. Davis, *Paradise to Prison: Studies in Genesis* (Grand Rapids: Baker, 1975), 232.

Isaac thus said to Jacob, "Now may God give you of the dew of heaven, and of the fatness of the earth, and an abundance of grain and new wine; may peoples serve you, and nations bow down to you; be master of your brothers, and may your mother's sons bow down to you. Cursed be those who curse you, and blessed be those who bless you" (Gen. 27:28–29). Later in the chapter, Isaac spoke to Esau, saying, "Behold, away from the fertility of the earth shall be your dwelling, and away from the dew of heaven from above. And by your sword you shall live, and your brother you shall serve; but it shall come about when you become restless, that you shall break his yoke from your neck" (vv. 39–40).

So we see from the very beginning that the place of Esau (and Edom) in God's program was determined. Esau would serve his younger brother. His people would be a violent people, and they would live in an unfertile land; but eventually they would break the yoke of bondage from off their necks. The history of Edom bears out the fulfillment of these prophecies.

This is where the Edomites came from. And their character and destiny were bound up with that of their father, Esau.

THE LOCATION OF EDOM

Genesis 27:39 prophetically declares that Esau's dwelling place would be "away from the fertility of the earth" and "away from the dew of heaven." Indeed, this proved to be the case. Esau settled in the rugged and desolate area directly south of the Dead Sea. There the Edomites established their nation. The capital of Edom was Sela, or Petra as it is better known. Simon's confession of Christ moved Jesus to declare him to be Peter, which means "rock" (Matt. 16:18). Petra is also from the Greek word for "rock" (*sela* is the Hebrew equivalent).[3] It was appropriately named, for it, like most of the settlements in Edom, was a rocky fortress. A first-person description of a visitor to Petra gives us an idea of the kind of land Edom was.

> This writer recently visited the ancient city of Petra, the Edomite capital, and was astounded. The only entrance into the city is a narrow gorge between towering cliffs 200 to 300 feet tall. A handful of men could undoubtedly protect this entrance against any invading army. The path twists and turns amidst the cliffs for over a mile until suddenly and unexpectedly you are confronted by the facade

3. J. A. Thompson, "Sela" in *The New Bible Dictionary,* ed. J. D. Douglas (Grand Rapids: Eerdmans, 1962), 1158.

of a building carved out of the rock. This building, commonly referred to as the Treasury, is but one of the many marvelous sights
to be seen within the city. There are still remains of a giant theatre
which once accommodated 2,000 people. A visitor to Petra can
still see the ruins of the triumphal arch, the marketplace, an old
temple and palace. As we left the city on our horses there was little
doubt left that overcoming the occupants of this city had to be
ordered and directed by God.[4]

The fortresses in the mountains and deserts of Edom were almost
inaccessible to invading armies. This tended to breed pride in the people.
They thought they were invincible, as is evident from the description in
the book of Obadiah.

The Petra treasury from above.
Courtesy of Wikimedia Commons, Openstockphotography.org

4. Gerald H. Twombly, *Major Themes from the Minor Prophets* (Winona Lake, IN.:
BMH Books, 1981), 52. Many will be familiar with some of the closing scenes of *Indiana
Jones and the Last Crusade*, which were filmed at Petra.

THE HISTORY OF EDOM

Early History

The history of the Edomites is a record of the fulfillment of Old Testament prophecies, beginning with the prophetic words of Genesis 25:23 and 27:39–40. We see almost continual hostility between Edom and Israel, even as there was hostility between Esau and Jacob. The struggle and warfare that ensued between the two nations was the result of Edom's failure to remember its place in God's plan.

We first come across the Edomites as a people and as a nation in the book of Numbers, many years after the passing of Jacob and Esau.[5] The Israelites had been in Egypt for some four hundred years until Moses led the people out of bondage through the miraculous work of God. Under Moses' leadership they began their return to their homeland of Canaan. After forty years of trials in the Sinai wilderness, the Israelite nation, probably more than two million in number,[6] finally came to the borders of Edom. In Numbers 20 we read:

> From Kadesh Moses then sent messengers to the king of Edom: "Thus your brother Israel has said, 'You know all the hardship that has befallen us; that our fathers went down to Egypt, and we stayed in Egypt a long time, and the Egyptians treated us and our fathers badly. But when we cried out to the Lord, He heard our voice and sent an angel and brought us out from Egypt; now behold, we are at Kadesh, a town on the edge of your territory. Please let us pass through your land. We will not pass through field or through vineyard; we will not even drink water from a well. We will go along the king's highway, not turning to the right or left, until we pass through your territory (vv. 14–17).

The Edomites' response to Israel's peaceful request was curt:

> Edom, however, said to him, "You shall not pass through us, or I will come out with the sword against you" (v. 18).

---

5. This would have been around 1405 B.C. according to Leon J. Wood, *A Survey of Israel's History* (Grand Rapids: Zondervan, 1970), 420.

6. Two million is a conservative estimate based on the fact that there were some 600,000 men over 20 years of age (Exod. 12:37; 38:26; Num. 1:45–46). See e.g., John J. Davis, *Moses and the Gods of Egypt* (Grand Rapids: Baker, 1972), 146–47, and Irving R. Jensen, *Numbers: Journey to God's Rest-Land* (Chicago: Moody, 1964), 17.

The Israelites then attempted to make it even easier for their Edomite brethren to grant them permission to pass through Edom by offering to stay on the highway and pay for any water their livestock might drink (v. 19). The Edomites refused again, and then "came out against [Israel] with a heavy force and with a strong hand. Thus Edom refused to allow Israel to pass through his territory; so Israel turned away from him" (vv. 20–21).

It is interesting that the Israelite messengers addressed the Edomites as brothers, saying, "Thus your brother Israel has said" (v. 14). This undoubtedly was a diplomatic way of making the request, but it also recognized the familial relationship between the two peoples. In spite of this, however, the Edomites refused the Israelites passage. The rocky relationship between the brothers Jacob and Esau had ended in peace (Gen. 33:1–17; 35:29), but now, centuries later, the competition and hatred that had marred their earlier relationship was renewed in their descendants.

More than three centuries later, Israel's first king, Saul (1043–1011 B.C.), fought against the Edomites. First Samuel 14:47 says, "Now when Saul had taken the kingdom over Israel, he fought against all his enemies on every side, against Moab, the sons of Ammon, Edom, the kings of Zobah, and the Philistines; and wherever he turned, he inflicted punishment." Thus at the beginning of the Hebrew monarchy, we find that Edom was considered an enemy, alongside the other nations that Saul put down.

Saul's successor David conquered Edom, and "all the Edomites became servants to David" (2 Sam. 8:14). David thus brought Edom into subjection to Israel, just as it had been prophesied (Gen. 27:40).

Edom was not content to serve his brother, however. The Edomite hostility toward Israel no doubt was heightened by David's apparent attempt to annihilate the Edomites, an incident alluded to in 1 Kings 11:15–16. When the opportunity came to retaliate during Solomon's reign, Hadad the Edomite led the revolt. While Hadad apparently created some trouble for Solomon, his rebellion was not successful (vv. 14–22).

A later rebellion proved to be much more successful for the Edomites. The reign of King Jehoram of Judah (848–841 B.C.) was a period of weakness in the southern kingdom. The Edomites took advantage of this situation and were able to gain their freedom from Israelite domination (2 Kings 8:20–22; 2 Chron. 21:8–10; cf. Gen. 27:40). Shortly after Edom's successful rebellion, a coalition of Philistines and Arabs invaded Judah and carried some of the people and possessions away from the king's house (2 Chron. 21:16–17). Edom not only gained a measure of freedom, but a major defeat also was inflicted upon Judah by this invading coalition. Apparently—and we can only say *apparently*—it was at this time that the Edomites rejoiced over the defeat of Judah, an event described in Obadiah 11:

> On the day that you stood aloof,
> On the day that strangers carried off his [Judah's] wealth,
> And foreigners entered his gate
> And cast lots for Jerusalem–
> You too were as one of them.

Obadiah 11 seems to be saying that the Edomites were standing by rejoicing over the defeat of Judah. It was probably shortly after Edom gained her freedom and Judah suffered this defeat that the book of Obadiah was written, somewhere around 845 B.C.[7]

Prophetic Preview

The Old Testament prophecies give us a prophetic preview of Edom's later history. As we have already seen, Obadiah is a declaration of divine judgment upon Edom. Obadiah was not the only prophet to speak of Edom's coming judgment, however. About eighty years after Obadiah, the prophet Amos wrote,

> Thus says the Lord,
> "For three transgressions of Edom and for four
> I will not revoke its punishment,
> Because he pursued his brother with the sword,
> While he stifled his compassion;
> His anger also tore continually,
> And he maintained his fury forever.
> So I will send fire upon Teman,
> And it will consume the citadels of Bozrah" (1:11–12).

Amos was pronouncing God's judgment on a number of nations. Among them was Edom, which would suffer complete destruction because of its unrelenting hostility toward "his brother" Israel.

---

7. The 845 B.C. date for Obadiah is often proposed by conservative scholars, although many also opt for a 585 or 586 date, connecting the defeat described in Obadiah with the Babylonian conquest of Jerusalem. See Gleason L. Archer Jr., *A Survey of Old Testament Introduction* (Chicago: Moody, 1974), 299–302, and Raymond B. Dillard and Tremper Longman III, *An Introduction to the Old Testament* (Grand Rapids: Zondervan, 1994), 386–87, for the various views.

Isaiah prophesied against Edom around 710 B.C.[8] In fact, Edom's coming judgment was set forth as an example of what happens to those who oppose God's chosen people (Isa. 34:5–17). The portrayal is one of utter desolation. As the following verses indicate, only animals would be left to inhabit the land of Edom.

> For my sword is satiated in heaven,
> Behold it shall descend for judgment upon Edom
> And upon the people whom I have devoted to destruction.
> The sword of the Lord is filled with blood,
> It is sated with fat, with the blood of lambs and goats,
> With the fat of the kidneys of rams.
> For the Lord has a sacrifice in Bozrah
> And a great slaughter in the land of Edom.
> Wild oxen shall also fall with them
> And young bulls with strong ones;
> Thus their land shall be soaked with blood,
> And their dust become greasy with fat.
> For the Lord has a day of vengeance,
> A year of recompense for the cause of Zion.
> Its streams will be turned into pitch,
> And its loose earth into brimstone,
> And its land will become burning pitch.
> It will not be quenched night or day;
> Its smoke will go up forever.
> From generation to generation it will be desolate;
> None will pass through it forever and ever.
> But pelican and hedgehog will possess it,
> And owl and raven will dwell in it.
>   (Isaiah 34:5–11a)

Jeremiah, prophesying in the seventh century B.C., added his words of judgment in Jeremiah 49:7–22. Jeremiah's prophecy against Edom closely parallels Obadiah 1–9. In fact, it seems almost certain that Jeremiah took Obadiah's words and adapted them for his own (and God's) purposes.[9] Jeremiah also wrote of Edom's doom in Lamentations 4:21–22 after the fall of Jerusalem in 586 B.C. Edom had rejoiced over Judah's fall,

8. Cf. Hobart E. Freeman, *An Introduction to the Old Testament Prophets* (Chicago: Moody, 1968), 193–94; Andrew E. Hill and John H. Walton, *A Survey of the Old Testament* (Grand Rapids: Zondervan, 2000), 420.

9. Archer, *Survey of Old Testament Introduction*, 301.

but the prophet contrasted Israel's glorious future with Edom's coming destruction.

Ezekiel also pronounced divine judgment on Edom, saying that God would bring vengeance upon the nation because Edom had acted in vengeance against Judah (Ezek. 25:12–14).

Obadiah remains, however, the earliest and most complete prophecy regarding Edom's destiny. We can summarize the message of Obadiah with the following outline.

1. Coming Destruction of Edom (vv. 1–9)

2. Causes of Edom's Destruction (vv. 10–14)

3. Coming Day of the Lord (vv. 15–21)

The first nine verses of Obadiah speak of the coming destruction of Edom. Verse 2 says, "Behold, I will make you small among the nations; you are greatly despised." The word "small" (*qaton*) also can be translated "younger."[10] It is as if the Lord were saying, "Even though you, Esau, are the oldest son, I am going to make you as though you were the younger." In verse 9, Obadiah wrote, "Then your mighty men will be dismayed, O Teman, so that everyone may be cut off from the mountain of Esau by [or, because of] slaughter." This declaration that the Edomites were going to be completely cut off meant that they were going to be annihilated as a people. As a nation and a people, Edom was going to cease to exist in history.

Obadiah 10–14 lists the causes of Edom's coming judgment. Verse 10 summarizes this section: "Because of violence to your brother Jacob, you will be covered with shame, and you will be cut off forever." Because of the violence done to Israel, Edom was going to be annihilated. The following verses spell out the violence Obadiah was referring to by listing the specific causes of Edom's judgment.

The last few verses of Obadiah (vv. 15–21) describe the coming day of the Lord. Judgment is going to come, not only upon Edom, but also upon all nations that oppose God and rebel against the Lord's plan for them. Obadiah announced, "For the day of the Lord draws near on all the nations. As you have done, it will be done to you. Your dealings will return on your own head" (v. 15). This is a divine principle, and it is the principle by which the Lord would judge Edom. Verse 19 adds, "Then those of the

---

10. "Small" is the more frequent designation of the word *qaton*; however, there may well be a double meaning here. See Leonard J. Coppes, "*qaton*," *TWOT*, 2:795.

Negev will possess the mountain of Esau, and those of the Shephelah the Philistine plain; also, possess the territory of Ephraim and the territory of Samaria. And Benjamin will possess Gilead." Of particular interest is the first part of this verse, which says, "Those of the Negev will possess the mountain of Esau." The Edomites would lose their land, displaced by another people.

The book of Obadiah pronounces God's judgment against Edom. Specifically, it says that Edom was going to be destroyed as a nation. The Edomites were going to lose their land. They were going to be supplanted and ultimately obliterated. Why? It was simply because they were not content with their place in God's plan!

Later History

Let us now go beyond the time of the writing of the book of Obadiah in the mid-ninth century B.C. and look at the subsequent history of Edom, for it is in the later history of Edom that we clearly see the fulfillment of Obadiah's prophecy.[11]

After the writing of the book of Obadiah, there was almost continual conflict between Edom and their Israelite neighbors until the fall of Jerusalem in 586 B.C. Of course, when we speak about Edom and God's judgment upon that nation, it certainly does not suggest that Israel was always a righteous people. In fact, the opposite was the case for most of the Old Testament era, which is why they too suffered divine judgment. The northern kingdom of Israel, which had split from the southern tribes in 931 B.C., was the first to experience God's judgment. It came at the hands of the Assyrians in 722 B.C. In 586 B.C. the southern kingdom of Judah fell to the Babylonians. Jerusalem was captured, and a large portion of the population was taken into captivity.

Where were the Edomites when Jerusalem was falling to the Babylonians? They were the cheerleaders. They were standing by, saying, "Burn it to the ground! Destroy it!" Psalm 137 was written during the Babylonian Exile. The psalmist lamented the suffering of the captives and in verse 7 called on God to remember the actions of the Edomites when Jerusalem fell. He wrote, "Remember, O Lord, against the sons of Edom

---

11. For brief overviews of Edom's later history, see John D. W. Watts, *Obadiah: A Critical Exegetical Commentary* (Grand Rapids: Eerdmans, 1969), 11–19; Leslie C. Allen, *The Books of Joel, Obadiah, Jonah and Micah* (Grand Rapids: Eerdmans, 1976), 129–31; and Archer, *Survey of Old Testament Introduction*, 303.

the day of Jerusalem, who said, "Raze it, raze it to its very foundation." The Edomites cheered on the conquerors. Seventy years later, however, Edom's despised brothers were back in the land of Palestine. With the fall of Babylon to the Medes and Persians, the captive Jews were allowed to return to their land and restore their nation (2 Chron. 36:22–23; Ezra 1:1–4).

The next hint we have in the Bible of Edom's circumstances is found in the book of Malachi. Malachi is not only the last book in our Old Testament but also the last Old Testament book to be written. It was written about 312 B.C. After a brief introduction, Malachi wrote:

> "I have loved you," says the Lord. But you say, "How have You loved us?" "Was not Esau Jacob's brother?" declares the Lord. "Yet I have loved Jacob; but I have hated Esau, and I have made his mountains a desolation, and appointed his inheritance for the jackals of the wilderness." Though Edom says, "We have been beaten down, but we will return and build up the ruins"; thus says the Lord of hosts, "They may build, but I will tear down; and men will call them the wicked territory, and the people toward whom the Lord is indignant forever." (1:2–4).

Malachi's words make it clear that by the end of the Old Testament era, the Edomites were no longer in the land of Edom. The Edomites are spoken of as still existing as a people, but they were no longer in their land. What had happened?

By this time a group of people called the Nabataeans had driven the Edomites out of their mountain strongholds. This was in direct fulfillment of Obadiah 19. So where were the Edomites at this time? Having been driven from their land, they had settled in an area in southern Judah that came to be called by the Greeks Idumaea.[12] The Edomite people from this time forth were known as Idumaeans. During the four-hundred-year period between the Old and the New Testaments, the Jews conquered the Idumaeans and forced the Old Testament law on them.[13] This did little more than add to the hostility between the two peoples.

When we come to the New Testament, Rome is in control of Palestine, as well as most of the Mediterranean region. The Jewish state had become subject to Rome in 63 B.C. In 47 B.C., about forty years before the birth of Christ, the Romans appointed an Idumaean ally as procurator (gover-

---

12. See, for example, the Book of 1 Maccabees 4:29 and 5:65.
13. F. F. Bruce, *Israel and the Nations* (Grand Rapids: Eerdmans, 1969), 171.

nor) of Judea. His name was Antipater. Antipater's son Herod eventually replaced his father and was declared king by his Roman sponsors. This ruler, known as Herod the Great, was an exceedingly wicked man. One writer described him as "an Idumaean in race and a Jew in religion" but a "heathen in practice and a monster in character."[14] He died shortly after Jesus' birth and after his own insane attempt to destroy the newborn King of the Jews (Matt. 2:1–20).

Herod the Great was succeeded in his governance of Palestine by three of his sons. Most prominent was Herod Antipas, who ruled as tetrarch of Galilee and Perea from 4 B.C. to A.D. 39. As an administrator he was no match for his father, but he shared many of the same character qualities. At one time he had sought to kill Jesus, and Jesus referred to him as "that fox" (Luke 13:31–32).

Upon Jesus' arrest, Pilate, the Roman governor of Judea, in an attempt to escape handling Jesus' case, sent him to Herod Antipas. Herod, who wanted entertainment as much as information, questioned Jesus at length, but Jesus did not answer him (Luke 23:1–12). The significance of Jesus' silence is not altogether clear. Could it be that because God already had said all He had to say to the Edomites that God the Son did not respond to this Edomite ruler?

In A.D. 66 the Jews rose up in rebellion against the Romans. That rebellion was dealt a deathblow in A.D. 70, when Jerusalem fell to the Roman general Titus. The Idumaeans joined in the rebellion, but they fared even worse than the Jews. The Jewish nation was in shambles, but the Jews themselves survived as a people. The same cannot be said for the Idumaeans, or Edomites. After A.D. 70 the Edomites ceased to exist as a distinct people. They disappeared from history. God's prophecy in the book of Obadiah was fulfilled.

THE LESSONS OF EDOM

It is a dangerous thing to forget one's place in God's plan. Indeed, it is both spiritually and physically dangerous to forget God's appointed place for us.

It is interesting to note that the Edomites were only doing what came naturally. After all, no nation wants to be in subjection to another people.

---

14. Merrill Unger, *Unger's Bible Dictionary* (Chicago: Moody, 1966), 471. Such an assessment of Herod's character is universal. Compare, for example, Merrill Tenney, *New Testament Times* (Grand Rapids: Eerdmans, 1965), 53–66; and F. F. Bruce, *New Testament History* (Garden City, NY: Anchor, Doubleday and Co., 1972), 13–24.

It is only natural to want to rebel against such subjugation; but what the Edomites had forgotten, or perhaps were ignorant of, was that they were not just rebelling against their overbearing younger "brother." They were rebelling against God and God's plan for them, which had been set forth in Scripture.

All of us have a place in God's plan. God has not specifically told each of us everything he wants us to do, but there are many, many responsibilities and many, many commands in the Bible that have been addressed to fathers, mothers, husbands, wives, children, employers, and employees. There are many specific and direct commands regarding both public and private aspects of our lives. Do we find ourselves rebelling against some of these commands? Do we find ourselves saying we do not want to be that kind of husband or that kind of wife or that kind of businessperson because it is too confining or too demanding? To ignore or reject what God has said in his Word is to rebel against God himself and to repeat the mistake of Edom.

PERSONAL APPLICATION

- What biblical commands define your place in God's plan?
- In what ways are you tempted to rebel against God's plan for you?
- Would you say that you are generally content with what God has given you?
- List three specific things you can do to become more content with your position in life.

FOR FURTHER STUDY

- Write a brief character sketch of Esau based on Genesis 25—27, 33, and 36. Use a concordance to find other references to him.
- Read an overview of Edom's history from one of the sources listed in footnote 11 or another book available to you.

2

Coming Destruction of Edom

Obadiah 1–9

THIS IS A TALE of two preachers. The first preacher was a young man who had grown up in a Christian home. It seemed natural for him to want to go into the pastoral ministry; so it was no surprise that after college he entered seminary. He had completed only one year of seminary, however, when he was diagnosed with a deadly form of cancer. After lengthy treatments that brought the disease into remission, he returned to seminary and completed his schooling. After graduation he accepted the pastorate of a small church. But soon the cancer returned. He continued his ministry as long as possible, but the cancer advanced rapidly and soon took his life.

The other preacher's life took a very different path. He was already a pastor when World War I broke out. The war changed him drastically. He found he had little to offer people who were suffering as a result of the bloody conflict. Indeed, his liberal religion did not give satisfactory answers to his own heartfelt needs, and he was forced to reexamine his faith. By the end of the war, he had begun preaching a very different message. It was a message that people began to take notice of when he published a commentary on the book of Romans. He left the pastorate and became a professor at a university. His fame spread, and soon students began to come from all over the world to sit under his teaching. His preeminence was such that a leading evangelical scholar declared that just watching this renowned theologian enter an auditorium was a religious experience. Unlike the first preacher, this man lived a long, honored, and fruitful life.

Which of these preachers was a success? Which one was truly successful—or were they both successful?

It is interesting how we so often evaluate people on the basis of accomplishments, influence, and fame. Yet in 1 Samuel 16:7, the Lord warned Samuel to avoid this very thing. He said, "God sees not as man sees, for man looks at the outward appearance, but the Lord looks at the heart." God looks beyond what is apparent and sometimes deceptive. The Lord looks at the attitude of the heart. The prophecy of Obadiah bears out this truth.

The book of Obadiah begins with God's passing sentence upon the nation of Edom. He then begins to set forth a divine evaluation of Edom's *attitude*. It is the attitude, what is in one's heart, that leads to actions. So it was for the Edomites. God pronounced judgment upon them because of their despicable attitude.

ANNOUNCEMENT OF JUDGMENT

> The vision of Obadiah. Thus says the Lord God concerning Edom—We have heard a report from the Lord, and an envoy has been sent among the nations saying, "Arise and let us go against her for battle"–Behold, I will make you small among the nations; you are greatly despised. (Obadiah 1–2)

The first two verses of Obadiah form the introduction to the book, with "the vision of Obadiah" being the title. We know nothing about the prophet Obadiah other than what we can discern from his name, which means "servant of the Lord," and from what he wrote in this small book. "Vision" is here probably used in the general sense of "divine communication."[1]

The prophet then immediately announced the word of the Lord concerning Edom, saying, "We have heard a report from the Lord." Rather than "report," the King James Version uses the word "rumor," which can be misleading. The Hebrew word simply means a factual report. The report heard from the Lord is that an "envoy has been sent among the nations." Obadiah does not explain what this means, and we can only guess. Many commentators suggest this was a human messenger sent out by one of Edom's enemies to stir up opposition to the nation.[2] It may well be, how-

---

1. David W. Baker, "Obadiah" in David W. Baker, T. Desmond Alexander, and Bruce K. Waltke, *Obadiah, Jonah and Micah* (Downer's Grove, IL: InterVarsity, 1988), 29; Leslie C. Allen, *The Books of Obadiah, Jonah and Micah*: New International Commentary on the Old Testament (Grand Rapids: Eerdmans, 1976), 144.

2. Baker, "Obadiah," 30.

ever, that this envoy was an angel God sent out to stir up the nations to rise up in judgment against Edom. Even as the book of Obadiah was being written, the Lord was using some means to move people to carry out his judgment on the Edomite nation.

God's sentence is continued in verse 2 with the words, "I will make you small among the nations; you are greatly despised." The Hebrew word for "small" literally means "insignificant." A secondary meaning is "younger."[3] It is an interesting choice of words, for the Edomites were the descendants of Esau, the older brother of Jacob (Israel). Jacob, however, was God's chosen. Here God is saying to Edom, "I am going to make you insignificant, or 'younger.'" The Edomites were not content to accept God's plan for them, as their conduct throughout the centuries revealed. They wanted to be like the older brother they were. God, however, was going to make them take the place of the younger brother. They were indeed greatly despised.

God thus introduced this smallest of the Old Testament books with a simple, straightforward announcement of his coming judgment upon the Edomites.

ATTITUDES WORTHY OF JUDGMENT

Following God's announcement of judgment in the introduction to Obadiah, the Lord began to set forth the faulty attitudes that brought Edom to this point. Verses 3–9 put forth those sinful attitudes in interesting terms.

Security in Fortresses

> "The arrogance of your heart has deceived you, you who live in the clefts of the rock, in the loftiness of your dwelling place, who say in your heart, 'Who will bring me down to earth?' "Though you build high like the eagle, though you set your nest among the stars, from there I will bring you down," declares the Lord. (Obadiah 3–4)

This is God speaking to Edom through Obadiah. The Hebrew word *zadon*, translated "arrogance," refers to pride or presumption.[4] The Edomites presumed to be secure in their fortresses. In fact, the Lord de-

---

3. Leonard J. Coppes, "*qaton*," TWOT, 2:795.
4. Leon J. Wood, "*zid*," TWOT, 1:239; BDB, 268.

scribed them as living in the "clefts of the rock." In the nation of Edom, there were a number of fortresses high in the mountains, built in such a way that a handful of men could hold off an entire army. Because of this, the Edomites became convinced that they were invincible. They presumed this in their hearts and deceived themselves into believing it.

They had deceived themselves to the point that they were willing to boast, "Who will bring me down to earth?" God's reply to that arrogant statement is found in verse 4. God declared, "Though you build high like the eagle, though you set your nest among the stars, from there I will bring you down." The Hebrew text can be accurately and literally translated, "I will cause you to be brought down."[5] God was going to use other people to humiliate and judge the nation of Edom rather than bring some direct, immediate judgment upon them himself. Edom would suffer at the hands of her enemies.

The problem was not Edom's fortresses. There is nothing wrong with fortresses. Neither is there anything wrong with defending oneself as a people. But Edom put her trust in military defenses rather than in the Lord, and there can be no ultimate security apart from the Lord (cf. Ps. 20:7).

Those who have no security in the Lord—that is, those who do not know the Lord and the security that comes from knowing him— quite often are inordinately concerned about physical security, about protecting themselves physically and financially. Indeed, even among Christians the insecurity of failing to fully trust in God has devastating consequences. Sadly, people will do almost anything to find security if they do not have it in the Lord. Edom found her security in her fortresses, and it was a great mistake.

Pride in Possessions

> If thieves came to you, if robbers by night—O how you will be ruined!–Would they not steal only until they had enough? If grape gatherers came to you, would they not leave some gleanings? O how Esau will be ransacked, and his hidden treasures searched out! (Obadiah 5–6)

Here God says that even if robbers came at night when the Edomites were not expecting them, the robbers would not take everything. The thief never takes every little thing. He takes what he can carry or what is

---

5. *BDB*, 433–34. The verb *yarad* is in the hiphil stem.

of value. Likewise, grape gatherers do not completely strip the vines. They leave some gleanings behind (cf. Deut. 24:21). With these illustrations the Lord was setting the stage for the dramatic contrast in verse 6.

In contrast to the illustrations in verse 5, Edom, or Esau,[6] was going to be completely devastated. Nothing would be left. Their "hidden treasures" would be utterly exposed and plundered.[7] "Nothing will remain hidden from the voracious conqueror. Israel's punishment, while great, will be partial in that a remnant will remain (e.g. Is. 10:20–22; Am. 3:12; 5:3; Zp. 2:3; 3:12–13). Not so Edom, who faces total eradication."[8] The "hidden treasures" are indicative of the Edomites' great pride in their possessions.[9] They were materialistic, and they paid the price for their materialism. They took pride in their possessions, rather than in God, because they did not know him.

Most of us would probably say, "We are Christians. We are certainly not materialistic." Is it not true, however, that all of us are infected with the materialism of our world to some extent? The degree to which we are materialistic can probably be measured by how we respond to loss. Would we be devastated if we lost our home? Would we be in despair if our life savings were suddenly taken from us? Do we take pride in the things we have and forget that they all belong to God? Edom's pride was in her possessions, and she had many valued possessions. God was not impressed.

Strength in Alliances

> "All the men allied with you will send you forth to the border, and the men at peace with you will deceive you and overpower you. They who eat your bread will set an ambush for you. (There is no understanding in him.)" (Obadiah 7)

---

6. "Esau" is used here for the nation of Edom, just as "Jacob" is used in verse 10 for the nation of Israel. This is a fairly common practice in Old Testament prophecy. Cf. W. Ward Gasque, "Obadiah" in *The International Bible Commentary with the New International Version*, ed. F. F. Bruce, (Grand Rapids: Zondervan, 1986), 915.

7. See *hapas* in *BDB*, 344.

8. Baker, "Obadiah," 34.

9. This is the only Old Testament usage of the word *maspon*, "hidden treasures." The word means that which is stored away as treasure. Cf. John E. Hartley, "*sapan*," *TWOT*, 2:774; *BDB*, 860–61. Edom's unique location gave rise to enormous wealth. See Joe Hellerman, "A Commentary on the Book of Obadiah" (Th.M. thesis, Talbot School of Theology, 1987), 58.

Edom not only had many possessions but also had many friends—or so it seemed. Those friends were a great source of strength for the nation. Even though the Edomites rested securely in their mountain fortresses, the nation itself was not large and not always militarily powerful. Their allies thus provided an additional reason for any nation that contemplated attacking Edom to have second thoughts. Those that would attack Edom would not be fighting Edom alone but Edom and her allies. Undoubtedly this added to the people's sense of security.

The great irony is that the very friends the Edomites had trusted would bring about their downfall. What is pictured in Obadiah 7 is not altogether clear in the Hebrew text, though the thought of betrayal by friends certainly is clear enough. Obadiah spoke of Edom's allies sending them "forth to the border." The picture seems to be this: The Edomites have gone to another nation seeking aid of some sort, presumably military aid. These "friends" have patted the Edomites on the back and escorted them to the border, promising them everything they have asked for. They appear to be good friends, but their promises are empty. They mean nothing.[10]

Some commentators see three different groups of people in Obadiah 7: "the men allied with you," "the men at peace with you," and "they who eat your bread."[11] It may be that the Lord was speaking of three different groups of people or three different countries, but it really matters little. He was simply talking about those who presented themselves as friends of Edom. It was their friends who would "deceive" Edom and "overpower" them, bringing about their downfall. We do not know exactly what allies turned on Edom and caused their fall. We know the Nabataeans eventually displaced them, but other nations may have been involved in the conquest of Edom. The Word of God simply tells us that Edom would be betrayed by those they trusted.

---

10. Robert Jamieson, A. R. Fausset, and David Brown (*A Commentary Critical, Experimental, and Practical on the Old and New Testaments* [Grand Rapids: Eerdmans, n.d.], 4:566) present this interpretation. Baker ("Obadiah," 34) and John D. W. Watts (*Obadiah: A Critical Exegetical Commentary* [Grand Rapids: Eerdmans, 1969], 51) suggest the Edomites were lured from their strongholds out to their unprotected border, where they were ambushed.

11. Paul R. Fink, "Obadiah" in *Liberty Bible Commentary*, ed. Edward E. Hindson and Woodrow Michael Kroll (Nashville: Nelson, 1982), 1719.

What was most shameful to the Edomites was that they would be completely taken by surprise and led into an "ambush." They would have no understanding of what was going on until it was too late.

Sometime ago a well-known television personality interviewed an actor who had experienced a number of tragedies in his life, including losing his wife in an accident. Asked what it was that had kept him going through these tough times, the actor replied, "It was my friends. I have some very good friends." A couple nights later, the same man interviewed a well-known criminal who had recently been paroled from prison. He asked this convicted felon the same question he had asked the actor: "What kept you going? What gave you hope during your years in prison?" The parolee replied, "If I didn't have Jesus Christ in my life, there would have been no hope. When I accepted Christ as my Savior and Lord while in prison, it changed my perspective on everything. It gave me a reason for living, and it didn't even matter if I got out of prison or not, because life was worth living."

These two men, who came from very different circumstances, make an interesting comparison. One had his friends; the other had Jesus Christ. There is nothing wrong with friends, of course. We all need friends, and the person who has them is rich indeed. Friends are a great source of comfort and encouragement, but they cannot bring peace of heart and mind. Only Christ can do that. He does not leave us, and he will never fail us. Friends can and will fail us. In the case of the Edomites, their friends brought their downfall.

Hope In Wisdom

> "Will I not on that day," declares the Lord, "destroy wise men from Edom and understanding from the mountain of Esau? Then your mighty men will be dismayed, O Teman, so that everyone may be cut off from the mountain of Esau by slaughter. (Obadiah 8–9)

In verse 8 the Lord announces the destruction of Edom's wise men. Apparently Edom was known throughout the ancient Near East for its wise people (cf. Jer. 49:7). In fact, one of Job's comforters was from Teman in southern Edom (Job 2:11). The wisdom of the Edomites was not enough to save them from God's judgment, however. Indeed, God declared that he would destroy the wise men of Edom along with the rest of the population.

Their wise men could not save them, and neither could their mighty men, or warriors. The Lord said, "Your mighty men will be dismayed, O Teman."[12] The Edomites were placing their hope in their own abilities rather than in the Lord. But their own resources would fail them. As David Baker puts it, "The very structures of society, in its constituent elements of economic well-being, wise rule and military security through armed force and international treaty, will topple."[13]

We see in Obadiah 9 a very specific prophecy of divine judgment. It declares that all the Edomites would be "cut off from the mountain of Esau by slaughter." "Cut off" (*karat*) is an expression that appears frequently in the Old Testament. Here it describes destruction by means of a violent act.[14] What is pictured here is a complete devastation of the Edomite nation. Everyone would be destroyed; the nation would be annihilated.

Verse 9 describes the destruction of Edom as being "by slaughter." These words do not give the means of judgment. The means is seen in the words "cut off," which describe a violent destruction. The words "by slaughter" can probably best be translated "for slaughter" or "because of slaughter."[15] It was *because* of their slaughter of others, their violent acts against their neighbors and particularly Israel, that they would be cut off, or annihilated. Edom lived by violence, and they would die by violence.

The Edomites had placed their hope in their own resources, their own abilities. They had rejected the Lord, so they had no place to turn but to themselves.

The British journalist Malcolm Muggeridge at one time was an unabashed liberal. Eventually, however, his thinking dramatically changed, and later in life he argued that liberalism as a worldview inevitably creates the exact opposite of what it sets out to accomplish.[16] Many Americans are

12. Teman, a major Edomite city, is used here for the whole country (cf. Watts, *Obadiah*, 51).

13. Baker, "Obadiah," 36.

14. Elmer B. Smick, "*karat*," *TWOT*, 1:456–57.

15. The Hebrew preposition *min*, which is attached to *qetel* (slaughter), can have this causal force (cf. Ronald J. Williams, *Hebrew Syntax: An Outline*, 2d ed. [Toronto: University of Toronto Press, 1976], 55). Both the NRSV and the NJB adopt this meaning and translate it "for," though both also attach the phrase to the beginning of verse 10, making it a part of the next sentence, a move that is unnecessary and unwarranted (cf. C. F. Keil and Franz Delitzsch, *Commentary on the Old Testament*, Vol. 10, [reprint, Grand Rapids: Eerdmans, 1977], 359–60).

16. "Human Utopia: The Great Liberal Death Wish," Christianity Today, 3 September 1982.

old enough to remember the war we lost back in the sixties—not Vietnam, but another war—the war on poverty. The Johnson administration declared "war on poverty." The result? Poverty rates rose steadily from that point on. Why? Because the policy that set out to alleviate poverty actually created poverty. The intention was noble, but the liberal worldview does not begin with a biblical view of humanity. It does not diagnose the cause of the problem correctly; thus the "solutions" only exacerbate the problems.

Scripture sets forth a similar principle that is illustrated by the plight of Edom. "Whoever exalts himself shall be humbled; and whoever humbles himself shall be exalted," Jesus said (Matt. 23:12). The one that seeks to elevate himself by his own resources brings about his own downfall. It was true of Edom, it is true of us as a nation, and it is true of us as individuals. When we rely solely upon our own resources, we guarantee our own destruction.

This was a devastating evaluation of Edom's attitude. The Edomites had chosen a course of independence from God. They had replaced him with fortresses, possessions, allies, and their own wisdom and power. Yet God said, "I will make you small among the nations; you are greatly despised" (v. 2). What is intriguing about God's declaration is that by every human measure Edom was a glowing success. What more could a people want than a sense of security, great wealth, good friends, and some measure of power and prestige? They were a success by the world's standard, but God judged them!

Today there is no Edom, and there are no Edomites. Obadiah's prophecy has been fulfilled. Edom is no more. But Edom's attitudes are still with us, and, sadly, Edom's attitudes can be found even in our churches. Too often, we evaluate ourselves and our churches by the world's yardstick. We place great importance on how much influence we have, how much we possess, how big we are, and who our friends are. When kept in proper perspective, these things have their place, but they can never replace the Lord. If we spent as much time seeking love, joy, peace, patience, self-control—the fruit of the Spirit—as we do seeking worldly success, the body of Christ would change the world.

God looks not on the outward appearance but on the heart. The true measure of success in God's sight is a proper attitude of the heart. It is a heart that looks to him alone for security, strength, and hope.

This chapter began with a description of two preachers. Who were those two preachers, and which one of them was a success? The young preacher who died shortly after beginning his ministry in a small church will forever be unknown to most of the world. Indeed, I knew him only because he was a seminary classmate of mine. Was he a success? Probably not by any worldly measure, but in God's eyes, I dare say he was tremendously successful.

The other preacher, who was proclaimed the greatest theologian of his era, was Karl Barth. He is the father of neo-orthodox theology, perhaps the greatest heresy of the twentieth century. By the world's measure, he was certainly a success. But was he a success by God's measure? Was he truly a spiritual success? I fear he fell far short.

PERSONAL APPLICATION

- What kind of people does the world idolize? What kind of person does God honor? List five character qualities that God values, and evaluate yourself in relation to each one.

- How many of your thoughts and efforts are directed at the things you own or hope to own? Does this hint at a degree of materialism? What can you do to counter this?

- Do you tend to see yourself as being self-sufficient? What is the potential danger in this?

- What do you tend to replace God with in your life? Make a list, and then use a concordance to find what the Bible says about each of these things.

FOR FURTHER STUDY

- Locate and read an article on materialism in a Christian magazine or encyclopedia. See, for example, the article in the *Encyclopedia of Biblical and Christian Ethics* edited by R. K. Harrison (Thomas Nelson Publishers).

- Find an article about a popular celebrity, and note the emphasis. What character traits are emphasized? For each trait mentioned or alluded to, find a Bible verse related to that characteristic. How would the article be different if God had written it?

- Which of the following biblical characters would be considered a success by the standards of today's world: Lot, Balaam, Joshua, Jeremiah? Which would God consider a success?

3

Causes of Edom's Destruction

Obadiah 10–14

MANY PEOPLE ARE CONCERNED about the portrayal of violence on television and in films because they are convinced that violent forms of entertainment will produce violent people. There certainly is some truth to that argument. People have been known to act out what they see on the television and movie screens, even to the point of committing murder. John Hinckley, who attempted to assassinate President Ronald Reagan, apparently was mimicking what he saw in the film *Taxi Driver*. Yes, the portrayal of violence and the glorifying of it in our motion picture and music industries is cause for concern. But consider this: Would the violence in entertainment even exist if we were not to some degree a violent people? In other words, is it our violent nature that produces the violent entertainment? Are we, in fact, a violent people? Probably most people would answer no to that question. But before we answer the question at all, we should think of this: the Edomites undoubtedly would have answered the question negatively as well, yet God judged them for their violence. Obadiah 10–14 gives us two historical warnings against violence.

THE CONSEQUENCES OF VIOLENCE

God first tells us through the prophet Obadiah about the consequences of violence. This served as a warning to the Edomites, but it serves as a warning to us as well. The warning is quite straightforward.

Because of violence to your brother Jacob, you will be covered with shame, and you will be cut off forever. (Obadiah 10)

Violence is the one sin that is singled out as being responsible for Edom's coming destruction. The violence of Edom was particularly evil because of whom it was directed toward. Edom had acted violently toward her "brother Jacob," that is, the Israelites, the Edomites' own relatives! As James Boice points out, "The particular horror of Edom's actions is that they were performed against those who were related to them in a special way . . . the two nations were brother nations and mistreatment of one by the other was particularly heinous because of this relationship."[1] We must remember, too, that the Israelites were God's specially chosen people. This made Edom's actions doubly wicked in God's sight.

What would be the results of their violence? In Obadiah 2 the prophet said the Edomites would be publicly disgraced in the eyes of the world, and indeed they were when they lost their land. Here the prophet said they would be "cut off forever." As noted in reference to verse 9, the expression "cut off" refers to destruction by a violent act.[2] In other words, what we see here is Edom being judged by the principle laid down later in verse 15, which states, "As you have done, it will be done to you." In essence, God is saying in verse 10, "You who have been violent in your actions against Israel will be destroyed by an act of violence. What you have done will be done to you!" Edom will reap what she has sown.

This verse makes it clear that Edom was guilty of violence against Jacob, or Israel, but what exactly was the nature of that violence? The Hebrew word used here (*chamas*) is used in the Old Testament only of *sinful* violence. This is an important distinction, for there are forms of violence that are not sinful. Warfare, for example, is violent but is not always sinful, for God has ordained warfare on various occasions. *Chamas* is not used of violent acts of nature. Natural disasters—earthquakes, storms, and so on—may be violent, but they are not sinful. The word is used of physical acts of violence, but interestingly enough, it is also used of language. One's language can be violent and sinful! In its broadest sense, the word *chamas* refers to "extreme wickedness," though

1. James Montgomery Boice, *The Minor Prophets: An Expositional Commentary* (Grand Rapids: Zondervan, 1983), 197.

2. Elmer B. Smick, "*karat*" *TWOT*, 1:456–57. Significantly, Jeffrey J. Niehaus adds that "the verb . . . when it occurs in the niphal (as here), always carries the sense of absolute termination" ("Obadiah" in *The Minor Prophets—An Exegetical and Expository Commentary*, ed. Thomas Edward McComiskey, Vol 2 [Grand Rapids: Baker, 1993], 527).

the violent nature of that wickedness is assumed.[3] It is the word used in Genesis 6:11 and 13 to describe the wickedness that brought the great flood upon the earth in Noah's day.

THE COURSE OF VIOLENCE

Verse 10 serves as a summary statement of Edom's sin. It states that Edom is guilty of violence and for that reason will be judged. Verses 11–14 go on to describe the particular acts of violence for which the nation will be judged. The descriptions of the four particular acts are enlightening.

Indifference to Another's Downfall

> On the day that you stood aloof, on the day that strangers carried off his wealth, and foreigners entered his gate and cast lots for Jerusalem—you too were as one of them. (Obadiah 11)

First, the violence of Edom is described as indifference to another's downfall. Obadiah probably was written about 845 B.C. In verse 11 the writer is looking back to a time prior to this, when Jerusalem was attacked and defeated and much of its wealth was carried off. This apparently is described in 2 Chronicles 21:12–17. During the reign of the wicked King Jehoram, a coalition of Arabs and Philistines attacked Judah and inflicted a significant defeat on the nation. It seems to be this event that Obadiah is describing.

The reference to casting "lots for Jerusalem" is explained by Gleason Archer: "As the city was being looted, lots were cast by the cooperating marauders to decide which quarter of the town would be granted to each contingent for the purposes of plunder."[4]

On that day, the Edomites "stood aloof." This Hebrew expression literally means they stood "on the other side."[5] The Edomites stood by, looking on as their Israelite brethren were being plundered. This is probably not to be taken literally, as though the Edomites were standing outside the walls of Jerusalem watching the attack. Rather, it is a picturesque way of describing their total indifference. This indifference toward the people of

---

3. R. Laird Harris, "*hamas*" *TWOT*, 1:297.

4. Gleason Archer, *A Survey of Old Testament Introduction* (Chicago: Moody, 1974), 300.

5. Cf. Carl Amerding, "Obadiah" in *The Expositor's Bible Commentary*, ed. Frank E. Gaebelein, Vol. 7 (Grand Rapids: Zondervan, 1985), 348 and C. F. Keil and Franz Delitzsch, *Commentary on the Old Testament*, Vol. 10 (reprint, Grand Rapids: Eerdmans, 1977), 361.

Judah was in reality an attitude of hostility. In fact, Obadiah goes on to say to the Edomites, "You too were as one of them."

The Edomites did not participate in that victory, and they did not fight against Jerusalem. They simply stood by and watched. Scripture tells us, however, that they were as one of those who *did* enter Jerusalem and carry off the wealth of the city. Edom's sin was that they just did not care about what happened to Jerusalem. They were indifferent. No matter how sinful the people of Israel and Judah were—and at times they were very sinful—they were still God's chosen people and the Edomites' brethren. The Edomites were not moved by any of this, however. Having recently engaged Judah in warfare themselves (2 Chron. 21:8–11), they simply did not care.

Are we a violent people? Perhaps we can best answer that question by answering another question: Are we indifferent toward the fallen and suffering? Paul Harvey often spoke of our "selective indignation." We are outraged by *certain* human rights violations—and properly so—but we ignore far greater offenses. We are rightly moved to action by the deplorable conditions in Somalia, but we ignore the wholesale slaughter of Christians in Sudan. Even as recently as the 1970s we managed to completely ignore the systematic extermination of over a million people by the Communist regime in Cambodia. It seems we *are* selective about what outrages us. It is almost as if we do not want to know what is going on in many places in the world because if we really knew we would have to act as if we were concerned when in fact we are not!

Of course, we cannot know everything, and we cannot help everyone, but we need to guard our attitude. It is easy to express our pious concern for the downtrodden while at the same time ignoring the plight of those in our very midst. Indifference toward another's downfall is equivalent to an act of violence.

Rejoicing Over Another's Downfall

> Do not gloat over your brother's day, the day of his misfortune. And do not rejoice over the sons of Judah in the day of their destruction; yes, do not boast in the day of their distress. (Obadiah 12)

There is a subtle shift between verses 11 and 12, and not all the versions reflect it. The change is in the verb tenses used. Verse 11 speaks of a past event. It looks back to something that has already happened before Obadiah wrote these words around 845 B.C. Verse 12 looks forward to something that is going to happen in the future. What it seems to describe is the fall of Jerusalem to the Babylonians in 586 B.C. In other words, Obadiah is prophesying an event some 250 years after his book was written (see "The Chronological Scope of Obadiah" following chapter 4). This prophecy takes the form of a warning to the Edomites, telling them what they should not do. At the same time, it is prophetic of what they would indeed do. This is simply a change from the past to the future and is cast in the style of a warning.[6] While this may be a bit confusing, the point should not be. The violence demonstrated by Edom is being described in terms of their rejoicing over the fall of Jerusalem, which at the time of Obadiah's writing was still future.

Obadiah says first of all, "Do not gloat over your brother's day." The word translated "gloat" (*thare'*) simply means to "look."[7] Because it is parallel to "rejoice" in the second sentence of the verse, it safely can be taken to mean something like "gaze upon with pleasure."[8] The Edomites rejoiced over the plight of the "sons of Judah."[9] They laughed within themselves. Yet God warned them not to gloat over the demise of Jerusalem.

We can imagine the Edomites' seeing what was happening to Jerusalem as the Babylonians marched into the city after a lengthy siege[10] and laid waste to it, destroying the temple in the process. The Edomites watched what was going on with a rather smug feeling, rejoicing within

6. The difference in the verb tenses is accurately reflected in the NASB and NIV among others but not in the KJV or NKJV. The verbs in verses 12–14 are all in what Gleason Archer calls the "normal negative-imperative construction" (*Encyclopedia of Bible Difficulties* [Grand Rapids: Zondervan, 1982], 298), that is, they are imperfects with the negative *'al*. They thus refer to actions still future (cf. David W. Baker, "Obadiah" in David W. Baker, T. Desmond Alexander, and Bruce K. Waltke, *Obadiah, Jonah and Micah* [Downer's Grove, IL: InterVarsity, 1988], 37 and E. B. Pusey, *The Minor Prophets—A Commentary* [Grand Rapids: Baker, 1950], 361). Many commentators take the verbs as expressing a wish or command without reference to any specific historical event (cf. Keil and Delitzsch, *Commentary on the Old Testmant*, 10:363). The view I have taken is also followed by Robert Jamieson, A. R. Fausset, and David Brown, *A Commentary Critical, Experimental, and Practical on the Old and New Testaments,* Vol. 4 (Grand Rapids: Eerdmans, n.d.), 567.

7. It comes from the word *raah* (*BDB*, 906ff.).

8. Cf. Jamieson, Fausset, and Brown, *A Commentary*, 567.

9. Note the use of the expression "sons of Judah" here rather than Jacob or Israel. The northern kingdom of Israel fell to the Assyrians in 722 B.C. By the time this prophecy of Jerusalem's fall was fulfilled, only the southern kingdom of Judah remained.

10. John C. Whitcomb argues convincingly that the siege lasted thirty months rather than the eighteen months often assumed (*Solomon to the Exile* [Grand Rapids: Baker, 1971], 150–51).

themselves that their hated brothers were getting what they deserved. They were probably boasting that they were not the ones suffering at the hands of the mighty Chaldean invaders.

The expression translated "boast" actually means to enlarge the mouth, or make great the mouth.[11] It suggests not only boasting of oneself but also insulting others, in this case, those who had fallen. As we saw in the introduction, Psalm 137 was written after the fall of Jerusalem in 586 B.C. The author pleads in verse 7, "Remember, O Lord, against the sons of Edom the day of Jerusalem, who said, 'Raze it, raze it, to its very foundation.'" The day Jerusalem fell the Edomites were standing by cheering on the Babylonians and encouraging them to level the city.

As the Edomites looked upon the destruction of the holy city, they must have been thinking that surely the tables were now turned. It was Edom that was loved and Jacob that was hated. From all outward appearances, that was exactly the case. It was Jacob's descendants who were being judged and Esau's descendants who were surviving and prospering. There is in this not only a warning to Edom, but a warning for us as well. We should never presume to make judgments based on outward appearances or present circumstances. Appearances can be deceiving, and circumstances can change rapidly.

Proverbs 17:5 says, "He who rejoices at calamity will not go unpunished." Proverbs 24:17 adds, "Do not rejoice when your enemy falls, and do not let your heart be glad when he stumbles." Edom rejoiced at the calamity of Judah and Jerusalem. Did God's chosen people deserve such calamity? Yes. Should Edom have rejoiced over it? No. The attitude of David is instructive. Many of David's psalms are what we call imprecatory psalms. They are prayers to God for the destruction of his enemies. Few of us would even dare offer this kind of prayer today, but there is nothing inherently wrong with such a prayer when properly motivated. David wanted to see divine justice carried out and God's name vindicated, and he prayed to that end that his enemies might be destroyed. Still, nowhere do we find David rejoicing over the destruction of his enemies. In fact, we find just the opposite (cf. 2 Sam. 1, 18). His was a proper biblical attitude. We can rightly rejoice in God's just actions, but another person's fall is nothing to be happy about, no matter how much that person might deserve it.

11. Cf. Amerding, "Obadiah," 349.

Reaping the Benefits of Another's Downfall

> Do not enter the gate of My people in the day of their disaster. Yes,
> you, do not gloat over their calamity in the day of their disaster. And
> do not loot their wealth in the day of their disaster. (Obadiah 13)

Edom reaped the benefits of Jerusalem's downfall. Following the Babylonian destruction of the city, the Edomites took advantage of the situation. They entered Jerusalem and looted the city. They carried off what they could find of value. They did not participate in the conquest—history tells us this—but they certainly took advantage of it. One might argue that if they had not done this, someone else would have. Undoubtedly, this is true, but it does not justify their actions.

The principle set forth here clearly has application to us today—especially those of us who are employed in the workplace. What happens when a person above us is fired for one reason or another? Sometimes we naturally reap the benefits of that person's downfall by being promoted into his or her position. We might benefit from the fact that we no longer have to work for or with that person. We might naturally benefit from the person's downfall, but we certainly should not seek to; and there is a big difference between those two things. It might not seem like a big difference, but it is. When we actively seek to benefit from someone else's plight, our actions are approaching violence. Sadly, this kind of "violence" is all too common. When someone loses his job, we see a scramble among those who have worked under him to promote themselves or benefit in some other way. The biblical principle is clear. We are not to seek to take advantage of someone else's downfall.

Protecting Self-Interests During Another's Downfall

> Do not stand at the fork of the road to cut down their fugitives;
> and do not imprison their survivors in the day of their distress.
> (Obadiah 14)

Verse 14 lists a fourth characteristic of violence. Edom's violence here is described as protecting her own interests amidst another's calamity. This is very similar to verse 13, which warns Edom, "Do not enter the gate . . . do not gloat . . . do not loot." Here Obadiah warns them not to "cut down their fugitives" and not to "imprison their survivors." Again, this is not just a warning but also a description of what would actually take place when Judah and Jerusalem fell to the Babylonians.

When the walls of Jerusalem were breached, a number of the city's inhabitants, including King Zedekiah, fled toward Jericho (2 Kings 25:4–5). But the Babylonian army soon overtook them and took them captive. Obadiah 14 indicates that the Edomites had a hand in the capture of these or other Israelites who were fleeing from the Babylonian invaders. They cut off their escape, captured them, and turned them over to the Babylonians.[12]

Why did the Edomites do this? It is not hard to imagine the Edomites' reasoning. The Babylonians were the greatest power on the face of the earth at that time. The campaign against Judah was just one of many such conquests. Edom saw an opportunity as the Israelites were trying to escape the onslaught. The Edomites cut off the escape and turned their brethren over to the Babylonian conquerors. They did not want to be caught harboring fugitives; and considering the power of Babylon, they probably wanted to make some points with this mighty empire. They were simply acting in their own best interests.

We have heard about similar things in our time, about people who witness crimes but will not cooperate with the police or come forward to testify because they do not want to get involved. It is not in *their* best interests to do so. To many people their own selfish interests are paramount. And in their minds, that justifies their refusal to get involved or to consider the interests and needs of others. To be concerned about one's own selfish interests to the exclusion of the welfare of others, however, is violence! And those who practice such things are violent people. They are in a sense as guilty as those who carry out the crime.

We would not normally consider the things described in Obadiah 11–14 as violent acts. In fact, in a relative sense, Edom's actions might not be considered all that heinous. They certainly did not act as wickedly as the Babylonians. They were not even as bad as many people and nations today. Indeed, if the Edomites were personally confronted with God's message of judgment, they might well have said, "We didn't do anything!" Yet God declared that because of their violence, they would be cut off forever.

12. The expression translated "imprison" in NASB can have the meaning of "hand over" or "deliver over," indicating the Edomites captured the fleeing Israelites and handed them over to the Babylonians (Joe Hellerman, "A Commentary on the Book of Obadiah." (Th.M. thesis, Talbot School of Theology, 1987], 91).

We tend to rank sins, considering some sins very bad, others not quite so bad, and still others hardly worth mentioning. Biblically, of course, some sins are worse than others. That is obvious from the fact that God declared some sins worthy of the death penalty, while others required some lesser punishment. But while some sins are more egregious than others, we must remember that *all* sins are detestable to God. Even those sins we might not consider very bad at all God calls acts of violence. We must always examine our attitudes and actions, not in light of the world's standards or relative to others, but in light of what God says in his holy Word.

PERSONAL APPLICATION

- Have you ever been guilty of violence toward others? If so, how could this have been avoided?

- Have you ever felt indifference toward the suffering of others? How can you develop greater sensitivity toward suffering people?

- Are you tempted to rejoice over the downfall of certain people? Why? How might resisting this temptation lead to ministry opportunities?

- Read Matthew 5:43–45 at least once a day for the next week. Consider memorizing these verses. Make a list of people who might be considered your enemies, and then list some positive, loving things you might do for them.

- Evaluate how much violence comes into your home by way of television or prerecorded movies. Determine how much, if any, is acceptable.

FOR FURTHER STUDY

- Do some reading about persecuted Christians through the ages, and note how they responded to those who mistreated them. Ruth Tucker's *From Jerusalem to Irian Jaya* (Zondervan) has several such accounts, and the classic *Fox's Book of Martyrs* also has many inspiring stories from the early days of the church up through the Reformation. The Voice of the Martyrs missionary organization is an excellent source of information on modern-day martyrs.

- Study some of the other nations surrounding Judah to learn how they treated the chosen people. In particular, read Jeremiah 46-51, Ezekiel 25-32, Amos 1-3, or Zephaniah 2. Was Edom the worst of Israel's enemies? What happened to the other nations?

4

The Coming Day of the Lord

Obadiah 15–21

J OHNNY BENCH, YOGI BERRA, Roy Campanella, Bill Dickey, and Mickey Cochrane—they are five of the greatest catchers ever to play the game of baseball, and all five are enshrined in the Baseball Hall of Fame in Cooperstown, New York. As great as these players were, however, not one of them ever led his league in hitting. That feat has been accomplished by a catcher only rarely in the history of the major leagues. Ernie Lombardi did it twice. Lombardi was a 230-pound catcher who was known perhaps as much for his huge nose (which earned him the nickname "Schnozz") as he was for his hitting prowess. He was a tremendous line-drive hitter, who compiled a lifetime batting average of .306—higher than that of such notables as Willie Mays, Pete Rose, and Hank Aaron—despite being notoriously slow afoot. He was the National League's Most Valuable Player in 1938.

Lombardi's baseball career ended after the 1947 season. He had every right to expect that he would one day be elected to baseball's hall of fame. But the honor never came. He watched as players of lesser stature entered the hall, and he waited until he gave up all hope of ever being so honored. The injustice consumed him and even drove him to an attempted suicide. Ernie Lombardi died a bitter man in 1977, never having come to grips with the injustice of not being properly honored for his accomplishments in baseball. Almost nine years later, in 1986, the veterans' committee of the Baseball Writer's Association of America elected Lombardi to the hall of fame.

Injustice is a hard thing to accept, perhaps especially by those who serve a just God. The psalmist Asaph wondered why the wicked prospered. He noted, "Behold, these are the wicked; and always at ease, they have increased in wealth" (Ps. 73:12). The prophet Habakkuk likewise questioned God's actions. He could not understand why a just and holy God would allow the Babylonians, people more wicked than his own, to judge Judah.

Obadiah assures us that God is just and that his justice will be realized. In this prophetic passage, we see two sides of God's justice.

GOD'S JUST RETRIBUTION

> For the day of the Lord draws near on all the nations. As you have done, it will be done to you. Your dealings will return on your own head. Because just as you drank on My holy mountain, all the nations will drink continually. They will drink and swallow and become as if they had never existed. (Obadiah 15–16)

The context of these verses is the fall of Jerusalem in 586 B.C. The nations, particularly Babylon and Edom, seemed to be getting away with their evil. God, however, declared that the future will be quite different, "for the day of the Lord draws near on all the nations." This is the earliest use of the expression "day of the Lord" in Scripture, but to what does the "day of the Lord" refer?

Many scholars believe this refers to a specific period of time in the future. Some limit it to the tribulation period; others define it as that period beginning with the rapture of the church and ending with the new heavens and new earth.[1] It seems best, however, to understand this expression as simply referring to an undefined time of divine judgment. "It is not a technical term in the sense that it always refers only to one event in God's plan. ["Day of the Lord"] is used to describe several events and is limited only by its mention in biblical revelation. Each appearance of [the expression] must be interpreted in its context to determine whether the prophet expected the immediate historical act of God or Yahweh's ultimate eschatological visitation."[2]

1. See J. Dwight Pentecost, *Things to Come* (Grand Rapids: Zondervan, 1958), 229–31, for the various views.

2. Richard L. Mayhue, "The Prophet's Watchword: Day of the Lord," *Grace Theological Journal*, Vol. 6, No. 2 (1985): 245. His position is further detailed in his unpublished doctoral dissertation under the same title (Th.D. diss., Grace Theological Seminary, 1981).

Having said this about the day of the Lord, it seems clear that in this context "day of the Lord" refers to the end-time judgment of the Gentile nations described in Matthew 25:31–46 (cf. Joel 3; Rev. 19:11–21). This will take place at the Lord's second advent and before the institution of his millennial kingdom.[3] Those nations that have demonstrated their rejection of Christ by their ill treatment of the Jewish people during the preceding tribulation period will be judged and consigned to eternal punishment.

The point here is that just as Edom would be judged and devastated, so God's judgment will eventually come upon all nations that oppose God and his chosen people. Edom's coming judgment thus foreshadowed the end-time judgment of the nations in the day of the Lord.

Following the warning of the coming day of the Lord, the prophet sets forth the divine principle of judgment: "As you have done, it will be done to you." The New Testament states the same principle in these words: "Whatever a man sows, this he will also reap" (Gal. 6:7). God's judgment is just. The punishment always fits the crime. This was true for Edom; it is true for nations; and it is true for individuals. Edom is a perfect example of God's just retribution as the following chart illustrates.

"As you have done, it will done to you" (Obadiah 15)

The Sin	The Consequences
"violence to your brother" (v. 10)	"you will be cut off forever" (v. 9)
"gloat . . . rejoice . . . boast" (v. 12)	"I will make you small . . . I will bring you down" (vv. 2, 4)
"enter the gate" (v. 13)	"send you forth" (v. 7)
"loot their wealth" (v. 13)	"ransacked . . . hidden treasures searched out" (v. 6)
"cut down their fugitives . . . imprison their survivors" (v. 14)	"Men allied with you will deceive you and overpower you" (v. 17)

Edom is here set forth as an example and a warning to others. The "you" in verse 16 refers to the Edomites.[4] They "drank on My holy moun-

---

3. See the chart, "The Chronological Scope of Obadiah," at the end of this chapter.

4. John D. W. Watts, *Obadiah: A Critical Exegetical Commentary* (Grand Rapids: Eerdmans, 1969), 57. Contrast this with Carl Amerding ("Obadiah" in *Expositor's Bible*

tain," the Lord said. There is probably a double meaning here, as indicated by the remainder of the verse. The Edomites had engaged in a drunken celebration over Jerusalem's fall, but what they had really drunk was the cup of God's wrath (cf. Isa. 51:17–23; Jer. 49:12). Indeed, all nations will "drink continually" from the cup of God's wrath until his wrath is poured out upon them.[5] The expression "drink continually" comes from a Hebrew root meaning "to swallow" or "talk wildly,"[6] clearly indicating the figure is one of drunkenness. Thus "the principle of retribution is applied within the figure of drunkenness. Edom and the nations have drunk and reveled on the mount of Jahweh's holiness. Theirs will be the fate of the drunkard: first incoherent blabbering and then unconsciousness. Perhaps the latter implies the drunkard's death as well."[7]

All who oppose God and his chosen people and revel in their seeming defeats will be utterly destroyed in the day of the Lord. Edom's fate should serve as a warning to any person or nation who would stand in opposition to the Creator and his plan.

What is described in Obadiah 15–16 is justice in light of eternity. We may never see justice in our earthly life, but we can take comfort in God's promise of ultimate justice. He will repay evil, and his retribution will be just.

GOD'S JUST RESTITUTION

Our justice system at its very best repays evil with punishment. God's justice also requires this, of course, but he does not stop there. He also sets all things right again, for in God's justice there is also restitution.

The Israelites could look at their long history, even in the time of Obadiah, and see much misery. They were God's chosen people, but it often seemed that God's blessing was a curse! It was their enemies, the Edomites and Babylonians, who seemed to prosper while they suffered. Obadiah

Commentary, ed. Frank Gaebelein, Vol. 7 [Grand Rapids: Zondervan, 1985], 353) and Leslie C. Allen (The Books of Obadiah, Jonah and Micah. New International Commentary on the Old Testament (Grand Rapids: Eerdmans, 1976], 162), who argue that "you" refers to Israel.

5. David W. Baker, "Obadiah" in David W. Baker, T. Desmond Alexander, and Bruce K. Waltke, Obadiah, Jonah and Micah (Downer's Grove, IL: InterVarsity, 1988), 39.

6. C. F. Keil and Franz Delitzsch, Commentary on the Old Testament, Vol. 10 (reprint, Grand Rapids: Eerdmans, 1977), 366.

7. Watts, Obadiah, 58.

thus not only pointed his people to a future judgment of God's enemies (vv. 15–16) but also to a future blessing for God's people (vv. 17–21).[8]

When will the conditions in verses 17–21 be realized? It seems clear that these verses, with the possible exception of verse 18, describe millennial blessings. It is during the thousand-year reign of Christ on earth following his glorious return that all the covenants God has made with Israel will be completely fulfilled. Thus here, as so often in the Old Testament, a future, glorious age for Israel is set forth as a source of hope and comfort for God's people.

Restoration of the People

> But on Mount Zion there will be those who escape, and it will be holy. And the house of Jacob will possess their possessions. (Obadiah 17)

In contrast to the nations who will be judged (v. 16), there will be some on Mount Zion (Jerusalem) who will escape. These will be that holy remnant of Israel, those who will be converted to Christ (Rom. 11:26) and enter his millennial kingdom. They will at that time "possess their possessions," or "inheritance" (NIV). The NJB aptly puts it; "The House of Jacob will recover what is rightfully theirs."

We see in this verse the fulfillment of two of God's covenants with Israel. First, because there will continue to be an escaped remnant, God's promise to David of an eternal kingdom for his posterity will be realized. The Davidic covenant (2 Sam. 7:12–16) guaranteed that the Jewish people will never be annihilated.

---

8. See Pentecost, *Things to Come*, 476. In contrast to those who would spiritualize these verses, Reformed scholar and pastor James Boice writes, "This must be taken literally. It must refer to a period of blessing of God on Israel as yet not seen. Some do not take the words this way. Either they say that the prophecies have been fulfilled by the humble regathering of the nation in Judah after the Babylonian exile, or they apply these promises of blessing to the church and view them as being fulfilled spiritually in these days. . . . I do not see how either of these views is possible. Above all, I do not see how the promises can be spiritualized. The only possible way to interpret the first two-thirds of Obadiah is to take the work literally. It deals with a literal nation, a literal period in history, and literal sins. Even the third part foretells a period of literal judgment on Edom, as we have seen. How is it that all of a sudden, between verses 16 and 17, we have to shift gears and say that the last few verses of Obadiah must be spiritualized? I do not see how this is possible" (*The Minor Prophets* [Grand Rapids: Zondervan, 1983], 206).

Second, in the promise that the "house of Jacob will possess their possessions," we see the fulfillment of that portion of the Abrahamic covenant that guaranteed Abraham's descendants a land forever (Gen. 12:1; 13:14–17).[9] The promise made to Abraham some four thousand years ago will be fulfilled in the future millennium. The fulfillment of this promise of an eternal inheritance is detailed in Obadiah 19–20.

Restoration of the Kingdom

> Then the house of Jacob will be a fire and the house of Joseph a flame; but the house of Esau will be as stubble. And they will set them on fire and consume them, so that there will be no survivor of the house of Esau," for the Lord has spoken. (Obadiah 18)

The nation of Israel had split into two separate nations in 931 B.C. (cf. 1 Kings 11–12)–Israel in the north, which consisted of ten of the twelve tribes of Israel, and Judah in the south, which consisted of the tribes of Judah and Benjamin. The Assyrians conquered the northern kingdom in 722 B.C. The northern kingdom was never reestablished. The southern kingdom of Judah lasted until the fall of Jerusalem in 586 B.C. The book of Obadiah was written before the fall of the northern kingdom, but it anticipated that fall as well as the collapse of Judah. While the captives of Judah would return after seventy years of exile to reestablish their nation, Obadiah looked beyond that return to a time when "Jacob" (Judah) and "Joseph" (Israel) would unite again and triumph over Edom.

Obadiah 18 indicates that the united people would have a part in the ultimate downfall of Edom. "They [Israel] will set them [Edom] on fire and consume them." This, of course, has already occurred. Today there is "no survivor of the house of Esau." It seems, therefore, that Obadiah has temporarily shifted his focus from the still future millennium in order to set Israel and Edom in contrast. Edom, which in Obadiah's time seemed very strong, would be burnt up; Israel, which was a defeated nation, would become a fire. While there would be no survivors in Edom, there would always be a remnant in Israel (v. 17). Historically, what is in view here is probably Israel's conquest of the Idumeans during the Maccabean era. During this period between the two Testaments, the Jews under John Hyrcanus subdued the Idumeans (Edomites) and forced the

---

9. Charles L. Feinberg, *The Minor Prophets* (Chicago: Moody, 1976), 129.

Old Testament law upon them, compelling them to be circumcised.[10] This was the beginning of the end for the Edomite people. After A.D. 70 there was "no survivor of the house of Esau."

Restoration of the Land

> Then those of the Negev will possess the mountain of Esau, and those of the Shephelah the Philistine plain; also, possess the territory of Ephraim and the territory of Samaria, and Benjamin will possess Gilead. And the exiles of this host of the sons of Israel, who are among the Canaanites as far as Zarephath, and the exiles of Jerusalem who are in Sepharad will possess the cities of the Negev. (Obadiah 19–20)

These verses detail Israel's taking possession of what is rightly theirs according to the Abrahamic covenant (Gen. 13:14–17; 15:18–21). The pronouns "they" and "theirs" refer to the people of Israel. What is described here is their possession of the land of promise in the millennial kingdom (cf. Zech. 14).

Obadiah pictures an expansion of the territory of Judah in every direction. Israelites living in the Negev, or south, will take possession of the mountain of Esau, thus moving east and farther to the south. Those of the "Shephelah," the low hills between the central highlands of Judah and the maritime plain, will move to the west and take possession of that plain along the Mediterranean, which was once the country of the Philistines. They will also occupy the territory of Ephraim, which encompasses the former Israelite kingdom to the north of Judah, along with its capital of Samaria. The small tribe of Benjamin will extend its borders eastward to Gilead, which lay on the other side of the Jordan River.

Furthermore, Obadiah declares that Israelites who had been exiled as far north as Zarephath between Tyre and Sidon, along with exiles living in Sepharad in western Asia Minor,[11] will have a part in possessing Israel's

---

10. F. F. Bruce, *Israel and the Nations* (Grand Rapids: Eerdmans, 1969), 171. Interestingly, Feinberg sees this as referring to an end-time judgment, when God's wrath will be executed "upon an Edom revived in prophetic times for this very judgment" (*Minor Prophets,* 129).

11. See David W. Baker, "Obadiah," 42, and Walter L. Baker, "Obadiah" in *The Bible Knowledge Commentary*, ed. John F. Walvoord and Roy B. Zuck, Vol. 1 (Wheaton, IL: Victor, 1985), 1458, for other suggestions.

promised land. The return to the land will be complete and the promises of God to Israel fulfilled when Christ rules.

Institution of Messianic Rule

> The deliverers will ascend Mount Zion to judge the mountain of Esau, and the kingdom will be the Lord's. (Obadiah 21).

Obadiah's prophecy concludes with a picture of the messianic kingdom under the rule of the Messiah. The land of Edom will be under Israelite dominion. "Mount Zion" will be the center of Christ's kingdom, and "deliverers" will from there "judge the mountain of Esau." The "deliverers," or "saviours" (KJV), will administrate Edom. While the Hebrew word means one who saves, rescues, or delivers,[12] the concept of deliverance can have many connotations.[13] Here the deliverers' responsibility is described as judging (*shapat*), the primary sense of which is "to exercise the processes of government."[14] The NIV translates the word "govern." The deliverers are apparently those saints from all ages who will be delegated governmental responsibilities under Christ during his millennial reign (cf. Matt. 19:28; 1 Cor. 6:2; Rev. 3:21; 20:6).[15]

While these "deliverers" will have numerous responsibilities in Christ's kingdom, the kingdom itself "will be the Lord's" (cf. Zech. 14:9). The word Obadiah used was *Yahweh*, the self-existent, everlasting, all-powerful Creator and Redeemer. In Revelation, John identifies this Lord with the Lord Jesus Christ, the King of Kings and Lord of Lords, who will reign on a restored earth with a restored Israel for a thousand years.[16] His kingdom not only will be greater than Edom's but also will be the most glorious kingdom ever! When he returns to establish that kingdom,

12. John E. Hartley, "*yasha*" *TWOT*, 1:414–16.

13. See Robert B. Girdlestone, *Synonyms of the Old Testament* (reprint, Grand Rapids: Eerdmans, 1976), 124–25.

14. Robert D. Culver, "*shapat*" *TWOT*, 2:947.

15. Pentecost, *Things to Come*, 498–501.

16. Bryan Beyer reminds us that "God is king already, but Obadiah looks ahead to a time when all the world will know, when every knee will bow to Him. The Christian looks for this kingdom, too, in the person of Jesus Christ, with whom he will one day reign" ("Obadiah" in Bryan Beyer and John Walton, *Bible Study Commentary: Obadiah, Jonah* [Grand Rapids: Zondervan, 1988], 26).

retribution will be meted out, but there also will be restitution, as God's promises to Israel are fulfilled, literally and completely.

It would have been easy for the Israelites of Obadiah's day to look at the wicked Edomites, who seemed to be prospering while they suffered, and declare, "There is no justice!" There is a warning here for all of us. We must never allow present circumstances to interpret God to us. How many times have we thought because of trying circumstances that God does not care about us, does not love us, or is not just? We must always allow the Bible to interpret God *and* our circumstances to us. We can never have a proper perspective on life apart from Scripture. Circumstances always change, and they will never be exactly to our liking as long as we live in this fallen world.

We serve a just God, and we are called upon to act justly in this world; yet until Christ comes we must be prepared to live with injustice, looking forward to that time when the Lord will make all things right.

PERSONAL APPLICATION

- Recall a time when you suffered an injustice. How did you respond? How should you have responded?

- What is divine justice? How does this compare to human concepts of justice? How is it relevant to your daily life?

- Find ten different Bible verses that speak of God's justice. How do they relate to circumstances you might face?

- List several things you can do for or say to someone who has been treated unjustly and seems to have no recourse.

- Read Obadiah 15–21, and list all the attributes of God either stated or implied in this passage. How, specifically, does each of these attributes offer you comfort or encouragement?

FOR FURTHER STUDY

- Read the article on "Day of the Lord" in the *Evangelical Dictionary of Theology* (2d ed., Baker Academic), or find a similar article in a Bible dictionary or encyclopedia.

- Read and outline the chapter on "God the Judge" in J. I. Packer's *Knowing God* (InterVarsity Press).

- Read the following passages that describe the future age of blessing for Israel, as well as any others you can find, and list the characteristics of that kingdom age: Psalm 2:7–9, 12; Isaiah 2; 9:1–7; 35; 65:8–10; Revelation 20:1–10. Some helpful resources for understanding the issues related to the millennial kingdom are: Herman Hoyt, *The End Times* (Moody Press); Charles C. Ryrie, *Basic Theology* (Victor Books); Donald K. Campbell and Jeffrey L. Townsend, *The Coming Millennial Kingdom* (Kregel Publishers). For a more popular discussion of the various views of the millennium, see Max Anders, *What You Need to Know About Bible Prophecy* (Thomas Nelson).

THE CHRONOLOGICAL SCOPE OF OBADIAH

Defeat of Jerusalem (845 B.C.)	Verse 11
Preexilic Period	Writing of Obadiah
Fall of Jerusalem (586 B.C.)	Verses 12–14
From Captivity (586 B.C.) to Fall of Jerusalem (A.D. 70)	Verses 2–9, 18
Present Age	
Rapture, Tribulation, Return of Christ	Verses 15–16
Millennium	Verses 17, 19–21

Exposition
of
Jonah

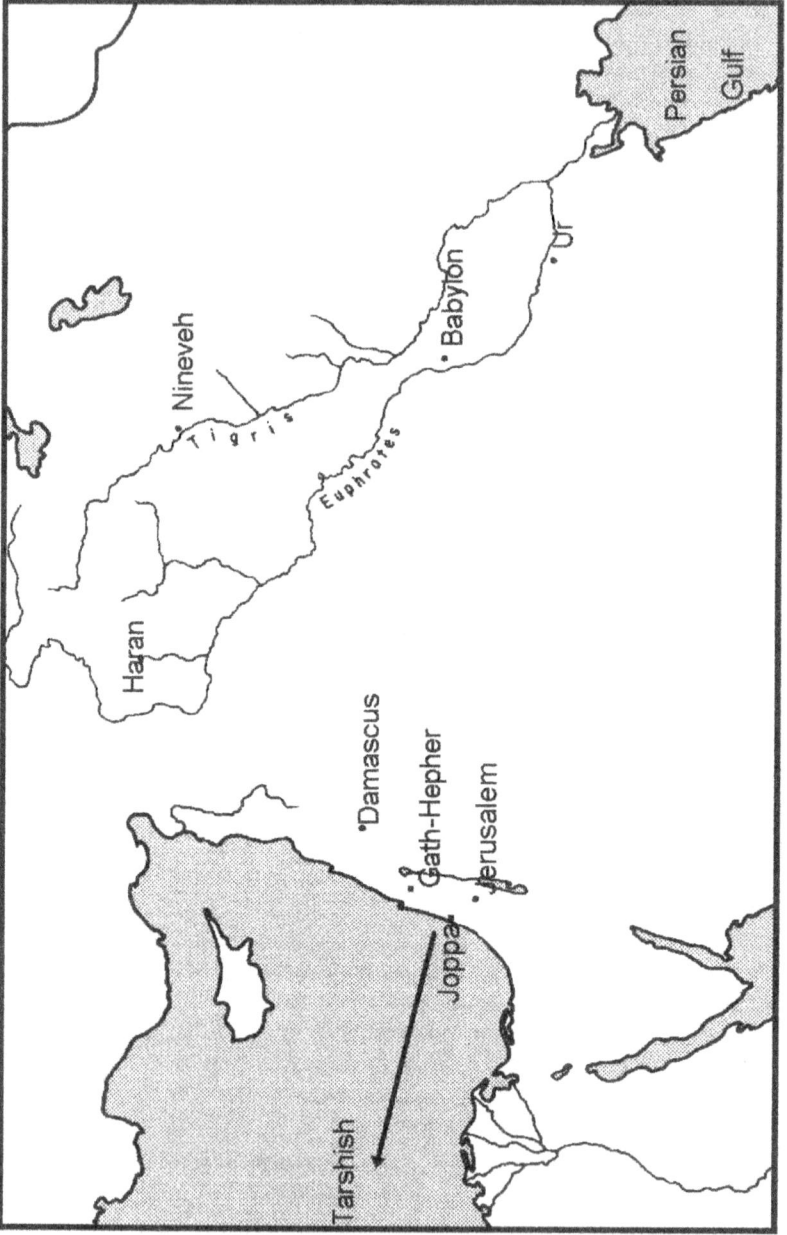

Persian Gulf

Ur

Babylon

Nineveh

Tigris

Euphrates

Haran

Damascus

Gath-Hepher

Jerusalem

Joppa

Tarshish

5

Introduction to Jonah

THE STORY OF JONAH is one of the best-known works in all of human literature. Even in this biblically illiterate era, there are few people who have not heard of this fascinating story. Sadly, however, most consider it no more than a fairy tale—an interesting, even humorous, tale of a man who was swallowed by a great fish and survived when he was spit out upon the dry land three days later. Sadder still is that many so-called biblical scholars have likewise relegated the book to the category of fable. It is not my purpose to defend the book of Jonah in all its details—that, I believe, has been adequately done by other Bible-believing scholars.[1] Suffice it to say, I am in total agreement with those who affirm the historical accuracy and divine inspiration of Jonah. My purpose is to expound this wonderful book—to set forth its glorious message in some detail—so that its familiar events become not merely curious occurrences of long ago but divinely ordained events that have relevance to us today.

Behind every amazing event in the Bible, there is a principle or truth to be learned. Behind every miracle there is a message to be learned and applied. That is certainly true of the book of Jonah. While many people know something about Jonah, most know little of what the book of Jonah is all about. There are, in reality, a number of amazing events in the book of Jonah, not just the familiar fish story. And if we dig deeply enough, we will find some important lessons behind those events.

One sure sign that Jonah is an important book and has some important lessons for us is the fact that it has been the focus of so many satanic

---

1. See, for example, Gleason Archer, *A Survey of Old Testament Introduction* (Chicago: Moody, 1974), 307–15; and Desmond Alexander, "Jonah" in David W. Baker, T. Desmond Alexander, and Bruce K. Waltke, *Obadiah, Jonah and Micah* (Downer's Grove, IL: InterVarsity, 1988), 51–77.

attacks! Perhaps more than any other book in the Bible, it has been attacked, ridiculed, and maligned. Surely, if there were nothing here of any relevance to us, Satan would not bother instigating such attacks. Yes, there are important lessons here. There are truths to learn and principles to apply.

The book of Jonah begins this way: "The word of the Lord came to Jonah the son of Amittai saying, 'Arise, go to Nineveh, the great city, and cry against it, for their wickedness has come up before Me.'" These opening verses raise two questions that we need to answer at the outset. Number one: Who is Jonah? And number two: What is the significance of Nineveh, this city to which he is told to go and preach?

WHO IS JONAH?

His Family and Prophetic Ministry

What do we know about Jonah aside from this book? The answer is, very little. Jonah is likely the author of this book since the information contained in it clearly must have come from him; and the book does reveal quite a bit about the prophet. But what do we know about his background? We are told that his name is Jonah, which means "dove,"[2] but there does not seem to be anything significant about that. We are told he was the son of Amittai, but the Bible tells us nothing about Amittai. In fact, what little we know about Jonah's background comes from one verse—2 Kings 14:25. Verses 23–24 set this verse in its context.

> In the fifteenth year of Amaziah the son of Joash king of Judah, Jeroboam the son of Joash king of Israel became king in Samaria, and reigned forty-one years. He did evil in the sight of the Lord; he did not depart from all the sins of Jeroboam the son of Nebat, which he made Israel sin. He restored the border of Israel from the entrance of Hamath as far as the Sea of the Arabah, according to the word of the Lord, the God of Israel, which He spoke through His servant Jonah the son of Amittai, the prophet, who was of Gath-hepher.

This is the only Old Testament mention of Jonah outside the book that bears his name. We are told that he was from Gath-hepher in Israel, the northern kingdom. This town was just west of the southern tip of the Sea of Galilee and only about three miles from a city we are familiar with—Nazareth. Jonah thus was from the Galilee area of Israel.

2. Archer, *Survey of Old Testament Introduction*, 307.

The only other thing we are told about Jonah here is this one prophecy he spoke. We know nothing of his original call to be a prophet as we do Isaiah, Jeremiah, and some others. We know only that he spoke this great prophecy of Israel's expansion eastward during the reign of Jeroboam II. The way he is introduced here would seem to indicate that Jonah was well known and well respected. We probably can assume that was the case, especially after this prophecy was fulfilled. But this is the only prophecy of Jonah's mentioned outside the book of Jonah. In fact, within the book of Jonah itself, there is only one prophecy—that in forty days the city of Nineveh would be overthrown—and that prophecy was never fulfilled. Although Jonah is included in the Minor Prophets, it is more a historical book than a prophetic one. There is just the one prophecy; the rest of the book is the historical record of what happened to Jonah.

The Bible does not paint a very flattering picture of this prophet. Indeed, he ran from God! He was a selfish, stubborn, disobedient man. Yet Jonah is one of only two writing prophets Jesus mentioned by name in the New Testament.

His Times

Jonah lived and prophesied during the reign of Jeroboam II, who ruled the northern kingdom from 793 to 753 B.C.[3] We do not know the exact time the events recorded in the book of Jonah occurred. It seems likely the book was written shortly after the events, perhaps around 760 B.C.[4] To put that into perspective, the northern kingdom's capital, Samaria, fell to the Assyrians in 722 B.C. So Jonah was prophesying about forty years before his own nation was conquered.

Jeroboam II was a wicked king, as were all of the northern kings. His reign, however, was a time of peace and prosperity, though it was a "fragile outward prosperity."[5] On the one hand, the wealthy lived lives of ease; on the other hand, there was much oppression of the poor. There was continuing and rampant idolatry and wickedness in the country, even as the nation prospered.[6] In fact, the nation of Israel was able to expand its territory to the east during Jeroboam's reign, as Jonah himself prophesied.

3. Leon J. Wood, *A Survey of Israel's History* (Grand Rapids: Zondervan, 1970), 325.

4. Archer, *Survey of Old Testament Introduction*, 308.

5. K. A. Kitchen, *The Bible in Its World* (Downer's Grove, IL: InterVarsity, 1978), 112.

6. Charles F. Pfeiffer, *An Outline of Old Testament History* (Chicago: Moody, 1960), 93.

Two other prophets—Amos and Hosea—ministered during this period, probably shortly after Jonah. A couple of passages from these two prophets give us an idea of the times in which Jonah lived.

> "I hate, I reject your festivals,
> Nor do I delight in your solemn assemblies.
> Even though you offer up to Me burnt offerings
>   and your grain offerings,
> I will not accept them;
> And I will not even look at the peace offerings of your fatlings.
> Take away from Me the noise of your songs;
> I will not even listen
>   to the sound of your harps.
> But let justice roll down like waters
> And righteousness like an ever-flowing stream.
> Did you present Me with sacrifices and grain offerings
>   in the wilderness for forty years, O house of Israel?
> You also carried along Sikkuth your king and Kiyyun, your images,
>   the star of your gods which you made for yourselves.
> Therefore, I will make you go into exile beyond Damascus,"
>   says the Lord, whose name is the God of hosts. (Amos 5:21–27)

Amos was saying that judgment was coming. Yes, the people seemed to have lives of ease. They enjoyed a prosperity they had never had before. There was peace all around, and the country was expanding. Everyone, at least those on the wealthy end of the spectrum, seemed to be getting along just fine. But inwardly this nation was corrupt, and judgment was coming.

Hosea said much the same thing; only he was more specific in one regard. Hosea 11 begins by recounting some of Israel's history. The prophet said God had called Israel out of Egypt. They were not going to go back to Egypt, however; they were going to go somewhere else. Through his prophet the Lord declared,

> They will not return to the land of Egypt;
> But Assyria—he will be their king
> Because they refused to return to Me.
> The sword will whirl against their cities,
> And will demolish their gate bars
> And consume them because of their counsels. (vv. 5–6)

No, they would not go back to Egypt, from which God had graciously and mercifully delivered them. They would go to Assyria. And that, of course, is exactly what happened in 722 B.C. The Assyrians conquered and decimated the land of Israel, and that is important to keep in mind as we move on to the next question. In summary, we can say that Jonah lived and prophesied in a time of prosperity but also in a time of decay, idolatry, and wickedness.

WHAT IS THE SIGNIFICANCE OF NINEVEH?

Why was God calling Jonah to go to Nineveh? Nineveh was located on the Tigris River. It was among the largest cities of the known world at that time and the principal city in the kingdom of Assyria. A generation after the time of Jonah, it was made the capital of Assyria by King Sennacherib.[7] As we saw, Hosea prophesied that this same Assyria would conquer Israel.

We must go all the way back to Genesis 10 to find the first mention of Nineveh in the Bible. There we are told that Nimrod built the city of Nineveh (v. 11). Thus it had a very long history. Nineveh was about 550 miles from Israel, as the crow flies. Of course, one did not travel in a straight line from Israel to Nineveh because the Arabian Desert lay between the two places. Travelers had to follow the so-called Fertile Crescent, which arced north of the desert. This would make the trip closer to 700 miles. Jonah was an Israelite, and a loyal Israelite, no doubt. As such, Jonah was presented with quite an interesting situation. God called him not just to prophesy against Assyria but also to personally take God's message of judgment to these enemies.

Something quite fascinating about Nineveh is that the city's name comes from the name of the goddess Ishtar, or Nina, which literally means "fish." The goddess Ishtar was depicted as a fish inside a womb.[8] It is interesting that Jonah, the man who would spend three days inside a fish, was commanded to go to the city whose primary goddess was represented by a fish inside a person.

During most of its existence, the Assyrian Kingdom was a very powerful and greatly feared kingdom. About eighty years before Jonah, the Assyrians had brought Israel into submission to them. King Jehu, the Israelite king, was forced to pay tribute to Assyria in 841 B.C., becoming a vassal of the Assyrian Empire. The Assyrians thus dominated Israel.

7. LaMoine F. DeVries, *Cities of the Biblical World* (Peabody, MA: Hendrickson, 1997), 33.

8. D. J. Wiseman, "Nineveh" in *The New Bible Dictionary*, ed. J. D. Douglas (Grand Rapids: Eerdmans, 1962), 888; DeVries, *Cities,* 31.

However, by Jonah's time, Assyria was having its own internal problems. The kingdom was occupied with a civil war and consequently was weakened and "relatively quiet."[9] Alexander described it as a period of decline.[10] As we saw, Jeroboam was able to expand his territory during this period. Assyria, therefore, did not have the grip on Israel it once had, but the Assyrians were still an enemy and a feared one. Consequently, they also were a greatly hated enemy, an enemy Israel could not forget and dared not take lightly. The Assyrians, in fact, probably were the most hated of any people of the ancient Near East, simply because they were the most brutal. The following quote from a British scholar of some years ago gives just a little flavor of what the Assyrians were like.

> The barbarities which followed the capture of a town would be almost incredible, were they not a subject of boast in the inscriptions which record them. Assurnatsir-pal's cruelties were especially revolting. Pyramids of human heads marked the path of the conqueror; boys and girls were burnt alive or reserved for a worse fate; men were impaled, flayed alive, blinded, or deprived of their hands and feet, of their ears and noses, while the women and children were carried into slavery, the captured city plundered and reduced to ashes, and the trees in its neighborhood cut down."[11]

Basically, the Assyrians annihilated the people and the places they conquered in the most cruel and brutal fashion, especially those who rebelled against them. Is it any wonder Jonah desired their destruction more than he desired their repentance?

OVERVIEW OF JONAH

The book of Jonah can be outlined as follows:

1. A Disobedient Prophet (1:1–3)

2. The Results of Disobedience (1:4–16)

3. A Prophet's Prayer (1:17–2:10)

4. A Great Awakening (3:1–10)

5. The Education of a Prophet (4:1–11)

9. Eugene Merrill, *An Historical Survey of the Old Testament* (Nutley, NJ: Craig, 1966), 270.

10. Alexander, "Jonah," 79

11. Quoted in Gerald H. Twombly, *Major Themes from the Minor Prophets* (Winona Lake, IN: BMH Books, 1981), 60.

Chapter 1 sets forth Jonah's disobedience and its results. We are told:

> But Jonah rose up to flee to Tarshish from the presence of the Lord. So he went down to Joppa, found a ship which was going to Tarshish, paid the fare and went down into it to go with them to Tarshish from the presence of the Lord. The Lord hurled a great wind on the sea and there was a great storm on the sea so that the ship was about to break up. (Jonah 1:3–4)

Jonah was from Gath-hepher in Galilee. He went down to Joppa on the seacoast to go to Tarshish. But where is Tarshish? Most scholars believe it was in southern Spain, far to the west. Nineveh, of course, was far to the east. Tarshish probably was the farthest point west anyone had ever heard of at that time.[12] Jonah, then, was making his exit in the exact opposite direction as fast and far as he could go. God, of course, brought a great storm upon the sea, and Jonah eventually admitted that he himself had caused the storm by his disobedience. The Lord, we are told, "appointed a great fish to swallow Jonah, and Jonah was in the stomach of the fish three days and three nights" (v. 17).

Chapter 2 recounts Jonah's repentance. Almost the entire chapter is given to the prayer Jonah prayed while in the belly of the fish. Often when we tell the story of Jonah, we skip over chapter 2. We can easily do that and still carry on the narrative. But in many ways chapter 2 is the key to the book of Jonah. Jonah's prayer and repentance is pivotal. Verse 1 says that Jonah prayed from the fish. We have no mention of him praying earlier. Then in verse 10, the fish vomited Jonah up onto the dry land at the Lord's command.

In chapter 3 we have Jonah's obedience and the resulting spiritual awakening. The first two verses are almost identical to the first two verses of the book. They read:

> Now the word of the Lord came to Jonah the second time, saying, "Arise, go to Nineveh the great city and proclaim to it the proclamation which I am going to tell you."

---

12. Cf. H. L. Ellison, "Jonah" in *Expositor's Bible Commentary*, ed. Frank E. Gaebelein, Vol. 7 (Grand Rapids: Zondervan, 1985), 369; Michael C. Griffiths, "Jonah" in *The International Bible Commentary*, ed. F. F. Bruce (Grand Rapids: Zondervan, 1986), 921; Alexander, "Obadiah," 99–100. Douglas Stuart (*Hosea–Jonah.* Word Biblical Commentary, Vol. 31 [Waco: Word, 1987], 451) argues that Tarshish is not a place name but a reference to the sea itself.

This time Jonah obeyed; he went to Nineveh and preached the message God gave to him. It was at this point that perhaps the greatest miracle in the book occurred. The population of an entire city—or if we understand it correctly, a group of three or four cities—repented and were converted. This was an amazing spiritual miracle. There was a great spiritual awakening among the Assyrians, and this was only forty years before those same Assyrians came and destroyed the kingdom of Israel. Jonah's preaching thus preserved the people who would later conquer his own people. This helps us understand why we find that Jonah was not at all pleased. *Chapter 4 then presents the lessons learned* through Jonah's negative attitudes.

THE LESSONS OF JONAH

Imagine an evangelist today seeing 120,000 people converted in a single campaign—and being angry about it! That was Jonah. He had some lessons to learn. We do not know whether Jonah learned those lessons or not. He does not tell us in the book, though we can assume by virtue of his having written the book that he did experience a real change of heart.

We can be thankful, however, for some very clear lessons for us in this fascinating book. Here are some of the major lessons from the book to ponder and dwell upon at the outset of our study of Jonah. First, *disobedience is always the result of selfishness*. One of Jonah's biggest problems was that he was selfish, and a selfish person simply will not be obedient to God. Why? A selfish person basically has made himself God, and self does not have anything in common with the true God.

A second major lesson from the book of Jonah is this: *God cares about people that we hate!* We might think that we do not really hate anybody, but if we were honest with ourselves, most of us would have to admit that there are certain people—maybe even certain groups of people—to whom we just do not feel the necessity of giving the gospel. We might not say that we hate them, but we are not doing anything for their spiritual benefit and do not intend to. God might state his point to Jonah this way: "You hate these Assyrians. I love them. They are brutal, cruel people; they are worthless as far as the rest of the world is concerned. But I love them; I care about them." That is the attitude we need to develop in our lives.

Finally, and maybe the overriding lesson of the book of Jonah is this: *God is sovereign*. John Whitcomb wrote, "The one, true, living God had the first and last word in this amazing book. *He*, not Jonah, was the principal person."[13] Jonah wrote this book, and it is about Jonah's experiences, but the

13. John C. Whitcomb, Notes accompanying the audio tape series "The Book of Jonah"

primary character in the book is, in reality, God. He is behind the scenes in a sense, but he is the one who is controlling Jonah; he is the one who is controlling the Assyrian Ninevites; he is the one controlling the weather; he is the one controlling the fish. Everything is under his control. And it is that—the sovereign, providential work of God—that is probably the most amazing aspect of this book. Think about it. God took a man who was disobedient, stubborn, and selfish—and remained so—and made him one of the greatest evangelists the world has ever seen. And Jonah was not even pleased about it! As we contemplate that, we should ask ourselves, "What can he do with us?" The answer is that he can do anything. He could take us even in our disobedience and bring about a great revival. Surely in our obedience, he can do far more than that. God can accomplish his plans through anybody, but he prefers to do it through obedient, submissive, godly people. Perhaps that is the greatest message of the book of Jonah.

PERSONAL APPLICATION

- List both the positive and negative traits you see in Jonah's life. Do you find any of these present in your life?

- Find Bible verses that might serve as a rebuke to Jonah's sinful attitudes.

- Read through Jonah, and note the attributes of God that are evident in the book. What effect, if any, did these attributes have on Jonah? What effect should they have on you personally?

- Think about the times in which Jonah lived. Are there parallels with our own society today? Is it true that a person is to some degree a product of his or her times? In what case might this be true of you?

FOR FURTHER STUDY

- Make a list of possible "problems" that critics might cite in attacking the historicity of the book of Jonah. Use some reference works to find suggested responses to these criticisms. The bibliography lists a number of helpful resources.

- Find other references to Assyria in the Old Testament. How are the Assyrians characterized in Scripture? What important biblical events involve Assyria?

- Read 1 Kings 13—17 to get an overview of life in the northern kingdom of Israel in the years surrounding Jonah's life and ministry.

(Hagerstown: Md.: Whitcomb Ministries, n.d.), 2.

6

A Disobedient Prophet

Jonah 1:1–3

THOMAS JACKSON EARNED THE nickname Stonewall at the battle of First Manassas, or Bull Run. Those who really knew him, however, probably were not surprised that Jackson stood like a stone wall while others were retreating. When the War Between the States broke out, Jackson was teaching mathematics at Virginia Military Institute in Lexington, Virginia. He was a decorated veteran of the Mexican War. He also was a man of great Christian character. He had even started a Sunday school in his church—a Sunday school for slaves. But probably above all else, he was known as a man who was committed to duty. If given an order, it was as good as done.

One humorous illustration of Jackson's commitment to duty comes from his early days of teaching at VMI. The superintendent of the school summoned Jackson to his office.

> Then, after pointing him to a chair, [the superintendent] disappeared to attend to an errand. Forgetting that Jackson had arrived precisely on time, and was awaiting his return, he fell into conversation with one of the teachers. Later, when he did remember, he surmised that Jackson had given up and retired to his room. Completely relaxed, he ate his supper and went to bed.
>
> But the next morning, when he stepped into his office, he was shocked to discover that Jackson was still ramrod straight in the same chair he had pointed him to the day before.
>
> "Sir," explained Jackson, "you told me to be seated yesterday and I'm following your orders."

The Superintendent stared. Then he laughed. Jackson had what
it takes to be a great soldier![1]

Jackson's action might seem a bit extreme perhaps, but he was doing
exactly what soldiers are expected to do—obey orders. It is amazing the
sacrifices that soldiers sometimes will make in order to obey orders—the
orders of a mere man. Why is it that we who serve the Creator of the
universe have so much difficulty obeying *his* commands? Both individu-
ally and corporately, it seems we Christians often struggle with obeying
our Commander's orders. That problem is not something that is limited
to this generation, however. In fact, we see it time and time again, even in
the lives of God's choice servants in the Bible. And Jonah, of course, is a
prime example.

The first three verses of Jonah describe the call of Jonah and Jonah's
response to that call. Rather than looking at it as mere history, let us look
at these verses in terms of two principles that are as applicable to us as
they were to Jonah.

GOD'S COMMANDS ARE REVEALED TO HIS SERVANTS

The word of the Lord came to Jonah the son of Amittai saying,
"Arise, go to Nineveh the great city and cry against it, for their
wickedness has come up before Me." (Jonah 1:1–2)

The first principle is that God's commands are always revealed to his servants. God does not hide his commands from us. He tells us everything
we need to know in order to serve and please him. It is not some great
mystery. We do not have to wait for some supernatural event. We know
what we need to know. Jonah, of course, did not enjoy the benefit of having the entire Bible as we do, so God spoke to him in a different manner,
but the principle is the same. God makes sure his servants know what
they need to know in order to serve him and please him.

Look at how God revealed his commands to Jonah. The text says,
"The word of the Lord came to Jonah" with this message. This very un-
conventional book begins in a very conventional way. As Alexander notes,
the expression "the word of the Lord came" is used over one hundred

---

1. Charles Ludwig, *Stonewall Jackson: Loved in the South; Admired in the North*
(Milford, MI: Mott Media, 1989), 95.

times in the Old Testament of God's communicating to his prophet.[2] It does not tell how God spoke to him. God spoke to his prophets through dreams, visions, and verbal communication, but that is not a matter of importance or concern here. This phrase points out the importance of the message, not the means by which it is given. It is not the messenger that is important but the message and the fact that it finds its source and authority in the Lord.

Whatever means God used to communicate to Jonah, he spoke very clearly and simply, saying, "Arise, go to Nineveh, the great city." The word "Arise" or its equivalent is not found in many translations.[3] The reason is that the particular Hebrew word used here is difficult to translate into English with any kind of meaning; so many versions simply leave it untranslated. But the Hebrew word is there, and it is best translated "arise." It does not mean that Jonah was sitting down or lying down. The word is used in Scripture of assuming one's office or responsibility or position, and it is used to emphasize the urgency of a situation.[4] God was saying to Jonah, "Get up, and get going. Assume the responsibility I am giving to you." It is difficult to convey all this with a single English word.

God simply told Jonah to go to "Nineveh the great city." The emphasis is on Jonah's going to the great city of Nineveh. The exact message he was to deliver is not revealed here, but it was clearly a message of judgment. As we saw in the last chapter, Nineveh was a great Assyrian city that at a later time became the capital of the Assyrian Empire. Thus, it was a very important city. In fact, the last verse of the book of Jonah tells us that there were at least 120,000 people in Nineveh. This has become a point of controversy, because archaeologists have unearthed the ancient city of Nineveh. They have measured its length and breadth and concluded that the city could not hold such a sizable population. Critics, of course, argue from this that the Bible data are wrong. In reality, it is the critics who are

2. Desmond Alexander, "Jonah" in David W. Baker, T. Desmond Alexander, and Bruce K. Waltke, *Obadiah, Jonah and Micah* (Downer's Grove, IL: InterVarsity, 1988), 97.

3. Cf. NIV, NRSV.

4. Leonard J. Coppes, "Qum," *TWOT*, 2:793; David J. Clark; Norm Mundhenk; Eugene A. Nida; and Brynmor F. Price, *A Handbook on the Books of Obadiah, Jonah, and Micah* (New York: United Bible Societies, 1993), 50; Joyce Baldwin, "Jonah" in *The Minor Prophets: An Exegetical and Expository Commentary*, ed. Thomas Edward McComisky, Vol. 2. (Grand Rapids: Baker, 1993), 552; Alexander, "Jonah," 98.

wrong. They have failed to understand that the reference here is *not* to the city of Nineveh proper.

Let me illustrate this before I explain it. When a friend of mine who lives in South Carolina goes to see her father, she tells me she is going to Chicago. I happen to know, however, that her father does not live within the city limits of Chicago. Is she lying to me? No. She is talking about the Chicago area—what we call Greater Chicago. That is exactly what is meant here by the expression "Nineveh the great city." It means *greater* Nineveh. We know that there was a complex of about four cities within this geographical area—Nineveh being one of them—which covered a wide area and had quite a large population. We must recognize that Jonah was not going merely to the city of Nineveh proper; he was going to Greater Nineveh—the city proper plus its environs.[5] It was perhaps the largest metropolitan area in the world of that day. It was, in fact "the capital" of the Gentile world.

This is the only example in all of the Old Testament of a prophet of God being sent to a heathen nation with a prophetic message. All the other prophets were sent to the people of Israel or the people of Judah. Jonah is the only one sent specifically to a heathen nation, and he was to go there with this urgent message of judgment. He was to cry out against the great city because of its wickedness. The urgency comes from the fact that this was a wicked city, and its wickedness had come up before the Lord. We find similar language back in Genesis 18:20–21. When God was speaking to Abraham about Sodom and Gomorrah, he spoke of their wickedness coming up before him. Literally, the expression here is that their wickedness had come "before my face."[6] It is a vivid way of expressing how offensive that wickedness is to God. It is good to remember that all wickedness, all sin, even those "little" sins that we commit, are before the face of God. The Assyrians were a very wicked, brutal, and cruel people. Nineveh also was the center of fertility cult worship, which was very debased goddess

5. Alexander, "Jonah," 55–59. See also Genesis 10:11–12, where we are told that Nimrod "went forth into Assyria, and built Nineveh and Rehoboth-Ir and Calah, and Resen between Nineveh and Calah; that is the great city." There the four cities Nimrod built are together called "the great city." I should point out that Douglas Stuart (*Hosea-Jonah*. Word Biblical Commentary, Vol. 31 [Waco: Word, 1987], 448) and C. F. Keil and Franz Delitzsch (*Commentary on the Old Testament*, Vol 10 [reprint, Grand Rapids: Eerdmans, n.d.], 391) are among those who believe "the great city" has more to do with its importance than its size.

6. Victor P. Hamilton, "Pana," *TWOT*, 2:728.

worship. But God knew all about it. It was in front of God's face and did not escape his notice.

This is a reminder to us that wickedness never escapes God's notice, but neither does it escape God's concern and compassion. That, as we shall see, is one of the main messages of the book of Jonah—God's compassion toward the wicked.

GOD'S COMMANDS DEMAND A RESPONSE

> But Jonah rose up to flee to Tarshish from the presence of the Lord. So he went down to Joppa, found a ship which was going to Tarshish, paid the fare, and went down into it to go with them to Tarshish from the presence of the Lord (Jonah 1:3).

God reveals his commands to his servants, but he also demands a response to his commands. Sadly, Jonah's response was not what it should have been. In fact, it was nothing like it should have been. We are told in verse 3, "Jonah rose up to flee to Tarshish from the presence of the Lord." Jonah's first and immediate response was disobedience. It was not submission; it was not prayer; it was not even indecisiveness. It was immediate disobedience. We might have expected more from a prophet of God. This, however, only proves what we already know—that even godly people can develop very ungodly attitudes. Even people who know God and know all about God can do ungodly things. Jonah's first and immediate response was disobedience—to flee to Tarshish.

Where is Tarshish? Even to this day there is not universal agreement on the location of Tarshish. We know for certain only that it was west on the Mediterranean Sea. Probably most scholars identify Tarshish as a Phoenician settlement in Spain, about 2000 miles away.[7] Where was Nineveh? It was about 550 miles east of Israel. Jonah headed west. If Tarshish was in Spain, it represented the most distant place known. Clearly, Jonah wanted to get as far away from Nineveh as he could. But it was not only Nineveh he was trying to get away from. He went down to Joppa, a seaport in Israel known today as Jaffa. At that time it was under Phoenician control. There he paid his fare to get onto a boat that was headed in the direction he wanted to go. Not only does this demonstrate his disobedience, but it also demonstrates his desperation. One

---

7. See note 12 in chapter 5.

thing the Israelites were *not* was a seafaring people. While there was a fishing industry on the Sea of Galilee, the Israelites generally avoided the Mediterranean. They did not have a navy, and while they had some ships during the reign of Solomon, they did not really have a lot of commerce by way of the sea. This only underscores the fact that Jonah was very anxious to flee.

Modern-day port of Joppa. Public domain photo from Wikipedia.

This raises a couple of questions. First, why did Jonah do this? Why did he flee for Tarshish? Obviously he was disobeying God, but twice the text says that he wanted to flee from "the presence of the Lord." This certainly seems like a strange thing for a prophet of God to try to do. After all, how does one flee from the presence of the Lord? Did Jonah really think that he could escape from God? Did he believe that he could hide from the Creator? I do not think that is what he had in mind. Later when he was talking to the sailors, he said, "I am a Hebrew, and I fear the Lord God of heaven who made the sea and the dry land" (v. 9). Jonah knew God had made the sea and the dry land. Obviously, if God made the sea, one cannot hide from such a powerful God by going out on the sea. Jonah did not think that he could actually hide from God.

We need to understand that God had a very unique relationship to Israel and the Israelites. God's earthly presence was manifested in Israel and specifically in Jerusalem. To flee from the presence of the Lord meant to flee from the land.[8] Jonah did not think he could hide from God. Rather he wanted to get away from God's presence, which was manifested in Israel. Jonah thought he might be able to avoid doing what God wanted him to do by avoiding the place of God's special presence! Fleeing from Israel was the best way he could express his total unwillingness to obey God.

In essence, Jonah was applying a useful principle in a negative way. A recovering alcoholic who is wise will stay away from the bar. Why? That is the place of temptation. If we have particular weaknesses, we are well advised to stay away from those places where the temptation is greatest. Jonah's thinking, it seems, was this: "If I can get out of Israel and away from God's presence, maybe I will not have to do what I do not want to do."

There is another question that is a key to this whole book in some regards, and it is this: Why did Jonah disobey? Was it fear? Was he afraid for his life? Certainly, it was not fear that motivated him. Later on, he told the sailors to throw him into the sea. He was not afraid to die. Did he not want to go because he hated the Assyrians? Let us think about that for a moment. The Assyrians were the Israelites' enemies. They were, as we have described, a very brutal people, and about eighty years before, in 841 B.C., a significant event had taken place involving Assyria and the northern kingdom of Israel. The Israelites had been forced to pay tribute to the Assyrians. In fact, the only picture from antiquity that we have of an Israelite king, the *only* depiction, comes from a stone called the Black Obelisk of Shalmaneser, which was unearthed in the Middle East in 1846. Shalmaneser III was the Assyrian king from 859 to 824 B.C. This obelisk is a large stone with a number of engraved drawings on it with accompanying descriptions. One of the panels on the obelisk pictures Israel's King Jehu on his knees with his face to the ground, bowing before Shalmaneser III. Behind him are Israelites bringing gifts to the Assyrian monarch.[9] Surely that picture or something similar to it was in Jonah's mind and in a lot of Israelites' minds when they thought of the Assyrians, for the event constituted a complete humiliation of the Israelite nation.

8. Keil and Delitzsch, *Commentary on the Old Testament,* 10:391. Cf. Charles L. Feinberg, *The Minor Prophets* (Chicago: Moody, 1990), 135.

9. J. A. Thompson's *The Bible and Archaeology* (Grand Rapids: Eerdmans, 1962), 129, has a nice picture of the obelisk, as does James B. Pritchard, ed., *The Ancient Near East: An Anthology of Texts and Pictures,* Vol. 1 (Princeton: Princeton University Press, 1958), panels 100a and 100b.

The Assyrians were still the Israelites' enemies, even though Assyria was in a period of decline at this point. Jonah, however, may have known that the empire's decline was going to be reversed and the Assyrians eventually would carry Israel into captivity. We know that Hosea, Jonah's contemporary, prophesied this, so it is possible that Jonah too was aware of what God had in store.

Given all this, did Jonah hate the Assyrians? Yes, it is clear that he did. Was that why he tried to flee? That may be part of the reason, but it is not the whole reason. Jonah himself gives us the reason, and it is found, not here, but over in Jonah 4:2. After Jonah had finally gone to Nineveh, preached God's message, and seen the massive repentance of the Ninevites, along with God's withdrawal of his threatened judgment, the prophet declared, "Please Lord, was not this what I said while I was still in my own country? Therefore in order to forestall this I fled to Tarshish, for I knew that You are a gracious and compassionate God, slow to anger and abundant in lovingkindness, and one who relents concerning calamity." Why did Jonah flee? He ran because he knew God is merciful. His message was one of judgment, which perhaps Jonah was delighted to preach, but he also knew God is merciful.

We will look at that verse in greater detail later, but it is a beautiful description of God and an accurate one. Jonah knew God. He knew what God is like. But he was not happy with the way God is. It seems strange, for sure, but do we not sometimes have similar thoughts? There is great danger in not being happy with what God does or who God is. If we are not pleased with who God is and what God does, it not only causes us to disobey God, but it also causes us to want to *change* God; and that is very dangerous. If we do not like the fact, or are not comfortable with the fact, that God judges the unsaved or that God judges those who have not heard the gospel, it is a great temptation to decide that God *will not* judge the unsaved. Some Christians might, in fact, be shocked at the number and at the names of some who call themselves evangelicals but now say they cannot accept the fact that God would judge some of these seemingly good people with eternal punishment. They have therefore simply declared that God is not going to do so.[10] In so doing, they are changing and molding God into what they want him to be.

10. See, for example, Clark H. Pinnock, "The Conditional View" in *Four Views on Hell*, ed. William Crockett (Grand Rapids: Zondervan, 1996), 135–66; and David L. Edwards and John Stott, *Evangelical Essentials: A Liberal-Evangelical Dialogue* (Downer's Grove,

Jonah's problem was just the opposite. He was not pleased that God is merciful! If we are uncomfortable with God's ways, it shows us how ignorant we are, or it shows us how sinful we are. Jonah was not ignorant. Jonah was sinful. He knew God. He knew what God is like, but he was not comfortable with that. He wanted God to be something else. He wanted God to be a God of justice and judgment but not a God of mercy and compassion.

When we decide to mold God into our way of thinking, we have taken the first step toward apostasy. We do not and cannot understand everything God does. We do not understand why he does some of the things he does. We do not understand why people go through some of the things they go through. But God is God, and he is sovereign. We cannot make him something that he is not.

God is the Creator. He is the sovereign Lord, and he is our Redeemer. He has graciously revealed to us everything in His Word we need to know in order to serve Him, in order to please him, in order to honor him. But he also demands that we respond to his commands with loving obedience—that we do not try to change who he is but rather respond to who he is. In regard to this kind of loving obedience, Jonah is not our guide; he is our warning. He is a warning that we are far too quick to go our own way and to demand that God do what we want him to do and be what we want him to be. If the prophet of God, who received direct revelation from God himself, can act that way, we can too. With regard to loving obedience and service to God, our guide is not Jonah but Christ, who "although He was a Son, He learned obedience from the things which He suffered" (Heb. 5:8). And his obedience was perfect.

PERSONAL APPLICATION

- Are there any revealed commands of God that you are failing to follow right now?

- Do you ever try to "hide" your sins or "flee from the presence of the Lord"? Read Psalm 32, and write down all the benefits of confession you find there.

- Do some self-evaluation and try to pinpoint any things about God and his will that make you uncomfortable. What can you do to change those feelings of discomfort?

IL: InterVarsity, 1988), 312–20.

- Do you ever insist that God do things your way? Think about the character of God, and consider why such an attitude is an affront to him.

- Do you consider yourself one who is eager to obey God's commands? If not, find someone you believe possesses such an obedient attitude, and discuss with that person the key(s) to a submissive attitude toward God's Word. Locate and memorize some Bible verses related to an obedient demeanor.

For Further Study

- Compare the call of Jonah (Jonah 1:1–2) with the calling of Isaiah (Isa. 6), Jeremiah (Jer. 1), and other Old Testament prophets. In what ways was the call of Jonah unique?

- Do some research on the archaeology, history, and religion of Nineveh and Assyria. The *International Standard Bible Encyclopedia* (Eerdmans), as well as sources listed in the bibliography of this book will provide interesting and useful information. Georges Roux's *Ancient Iraq* (Penguin) gives a lengthy and complete treatment of ancient Assyria.

- Using a map of the ancient Near East and the Mediterranean world, note the approximate locations of Nineveh, Joppa, Tarshish, and Jonah's hometown of Gath-hepher. Use the scale to determine the approximate distances from one place to the other. Find the locations of these places on a modern-day map as well.

7

The Results of Disobedience

Jonah 1:4–16

DISOBEDIENCE ALWAYS HAS CONSEQUENCES. It certainly has consequences for a child in a family. But it also has consequences for both children and adults in the family of God. Those consequences can be very painful, and they can affect others beside the guilty party. There is something far worse than suffering the consequences of disobedience, however, and that is being allowed to continue unabated in disobedience. We can be thankful if we had parents who loved us enough to discipline us rather than allow us to continue on in rebellion and disobedience. Likewise, we can be thankful for a God who also loves us enough to discipline us in his own unique ways.

Jonah had disobeyed the clear command of God to go to Nineveh. God could have let him go. He could have found somebody else who might have been willing to obey his command, but he did not. God loved Jonah enough that he would not allow him to continue in his disobedience, and that meant that divine discipline must be brought to bear upon God's prophet. These verses describe the results of Jonah's disobedience in relation to him and others.

RESULTS FOR OTHERS

The Lord hurled a great wind on the sea and there was a great storm on the sea so that the ship was about to break up. Then the sailors became afraid and every man cried to his god, and they

66

threw the cargo which was in the ship into the sea to lighten it for them. But Jonah had gone below into the hold of the ship, lain down and fallen sound asleep. So the captain approached him and said, "How is it that you are sleeping? Get up, call on your god. Perhaps your god will be concerned about us so that we will not perish." (Jonah 1:4–6).

Sadly, in verses 4 to 6 we see that Jonah's disobedience affected other people, namely, the sailors on the ship. Jonah had gone down to Joppa in disobedience to God. He had gotten onto the boat and set sail for Tarshish in the western Mediterranean. Verse 4 tells us, "The Lord hurled a great wind on the sea and there was a great storm on the sea so that the ship was about to break up," or be torn apart. The Hebrew language has a way of emphasizing certain things. In this particular verse, the emphasis is on "the Lord."[1] It is saying, "The Lord—He is the One" who hurled this storm onto the sea. It is making a point of emphasizing that this storm came directly from the hand of the Lord in response to Jonah's disobedience. It was a particularly severe storm, and one that was unexpected.[2]

The first time I flew on a commercial airplane, I did not know quite what to expect. Once the plane was off the ground and up in the air, I began to feel comfortable. Then the plane seemed to hit a speed bump, and my heart began to race. I did not know whether this was normal or something to be alarmed about. Almost automatically I looked at the flight attendants, and I noticed they were going about their business normally, so I concluded that this was a normal thing and was nothing to be frightened about. As we look at the sailors on Jonah's ship, we see quite a different reaction. These were experienced sailors; yet the text tells us that they "became afraid." This was a significant storm. The sailors feared for their lives. Undoubtedly they had been in many storms before, but apparently nothing like this.

These sailors probably were Phoenicians, who were known for their seafaring ways. It is possible some of the sailors could have come from other countries, but they were all polytheistic. They believed in many gods and goddesses. When they realized that this situation was beyond

---

1. The word Yahweh ("Lord") appears first in the Hebrew text.

2. David Clark, Norm Mundhenk, Eugene A. Nida, and Brynmor F. Price, *A Handbook on the Books of Obadiah, Jonah, and Micah* (New York: United Bible Societies, 1993), 54; cf. Joyce Baldwin, "Jonah" in *The Minor Prophets: An Exegetical and Expository Commentary*, ed. Thomas Edward McComisky, Vol. 2 (Grand Rapids: Baker, 1993), 556.

their control, they began to pray to their various gods and goddesses. Perhaps they prayed to particular gods that they had worshiped in their hometowns, or maybe they prayed to gods they thought controlled the sea or the winds, but they all began to pray. They also began to throw the cargo that was in the ship into the sea in order to lighten the vessel. Thus they were doing two things: they were praying on the one hand and working on the other hand, doing everything they could to save themselves. The lightening of the ship's load was to make the ship ride higher in the water so that it would be less likely to be swamped by the waves. As they worked, they prayed, for they were in great fear. This was no ordinary storm. It was a life threatening one, and they recognized that.

Notice in verse 5, however, the tremendous contrast between these sailors and Jonah. Where was Jonah? We are told that he had "gone below into the hold of the ship, lain down and fallen sound asleep." "Sound asleep" is an expression that means a very deep sleep.[3] It is used elsewhere of God's bringing a sound sleep upon someone (cf. Gen. 15:12; 1 Sam. 26:12). Jonah was peacefully sleeping in the hold of the ship. The contrast could not be greater. We have the sailors on the one hand, praying and working like mad to save themselves, while Jonah on the other hand was neither praying nor working. He was sleeping.

This calls to mind a similar scene in the New Testament on another sea, the Sea of Galilee. The disciples were out in a boat with Jesus, and a storm came up. The disciples feared for their lives, but where was Jesus? He was in the same place Jonah was. He was sleeping. While those two instances might seem similar, the contrast between Jonah and Jesus is this. Jesus was sleeping because he had nothing to worry about. He was in complete control, and he proved it moments later when he arose and told the sea and the wind to be calm, and they instantly became quiet (Matt. 8:23–27). Jonah, however, apparently was sleeping because he did not care.

Verse 6 says, "The captain approached him and said, 'How is it that you are sleeping?'" Apparently, the captain did not go looking for Jonah. He was probably in the midst of doing what he could to save the ship, when he stumbled upon the sleeping prophet.[4] It must have been an amazing sight in the middle of this storm to look down and find this man

3. *BDB*, 922.

4. "The use of the verb 'came upon' (NEB) suggests an element of chance in the encounter between the captain and Jonah" (Clark et al, *A Handbook,* 58).

sleeping so soundly. The surprised captain told Jonah to get up and pray to his god. "Call on your god. Perhaps your god will be concerned about us so that we will not perish," he said. So far, the sailors' prayers had done no good.

Jonah thus was commanded to pray to his God in hope of saving this ship and all the lives aboard it. Here is the great irony. Jonah had not been praying and apparently did not pray—even when commanded—yet Jonah was the only one on board who knew the true God, the only God who could save them! The sailors were praying to their gods, but what good does it do to pray to a nonexistent god? The only God who could save them was the God Jonah knew, and Jonah was not praying. In fact, Jonah was not doing anything, though he was the very cause for the storm's coming upon them.

Here is an important point. When we disobey God and go our own way, we bring hardship not only upon ourselves but upon others as well. These sailors did not ask for what they were going through, but they were going through it nonetheless because of Jonah's disobedience. Likewise, our disobedience to God brings hardship upon others, as well as ourselves. That is nowhere more evident than in our families. When the husband does not love his wife as he is commanded to do, it affects him, his wife, his children, and who knows how many other people. When the wife does not submit to her husband as she is commanded to do, it affects her, her husband, her children, and who knows how many other people. When children do not obey and respect their parents as they are commanded to do, it affects themselves, their parents, and who knows how many other people and even other generations. Jonah's disobedience affected many other people. Sadly, in Jonah's case, it was unbelievers, who desperately needed to hear the truth.

RESULTS FOR JONAH

Humiliation

Each man said to his mate, "Come, let us cast lots so we may learn on whose account this calamity has struck us." So they cast lots and the lot fell on Jonah. Then they said to him, "Tell us, now! On whose account has this calamity struck us? What is your occupation? And where do you come from? What is your country? From what people are you?" He said to them, "I am a Hebrew, and I fear the Lord God of heaven who made the sea and the dry land."

Then the men became extremely frightened and they said to him, "How could you do this?" For the men knew that he was fleeing from the presence of the Lord, because he had told them. (Jonah 1:7–10)

Jonah's disobedience certainly had consequences for himself. In verses 7–10 we see that as a result of his disobedience, he was brought to complete and utter humiliation. Verse 7 says that the sailors decided to cast lots to see who was to blame for the storm that had come upon them. "So they cast lots and the lot fell on Jonah." What were they doing? Probably the fierceness of this storm and the failure of their own prayers convinced them that there was not much they could do other than find the cause of the storm. So they began to cast lots. This was simply a superstition that they followed, but they believed that if they followed this procedure of casting lots, it would tell them the cause of their trouble. Oddly enough, the lot fell on Jonah.

What can we make of this? As we have said before, the main character in this book is not Jonah but God. We can only say that God sovereignly worked through these sailors' pagan superstitions—or in spite of their superstitions—to point them in the right direction. This does not justify their method or give any credence to it. God simply took what these pagan sailors superstitiously believed and used it to direct them to Jonah.

When the lot fell on Jonah, the sailors said to him, "Tell us, now! On whose account has this calamity struck us?" Did the lots not just tell them that? They were probably like anybody else who is superstitious. Superstition does not give much assurance, so they sought some confirmation. Maybe they thought the lot simply pointed them to the one who could answer their question. At any rate, they asked him who was responsible for this calamity. Then they asked him another question: "What is your occupation?" The idea here is probably, "What is your business on this ship?"[5] This is followed in rapid-fire succession by more questions: "Where do you come from? What is your country? From what people are you?" Remember that this interview, as it were, was taking place in the midst of a severe storm. It was not a formal interview with plenty of time to formulate questions. It appears the sailors were shouting out their questions as they came to mind.

---

5. Desmond Alexander, "Jonah" in David W. Baker, T. Desmond Alexander, and Bruce K. Waltke, *Obadiah, Jonah and Micah* (Downer's Grove, IL: InterVarsity, 1988), 105.

They were trying to get to the bottom of this, trying desperately to find something that might save them.[6] They wanted answers.

Jonah gave them some answers in verse 9. He began by telling them he was a Hebrew. "Hebrew" was the term used by Israel's neighbors for the Israelites (cf. 1 Sam. 4:6, 9; 14:11).[7] Jonah then declared, "I fear the Lord God of heaven who made the sea and the dry land." This assertion by Jonah sounds quite hollow. He claimed to fear the Lord, but obviously he did not fear the Lord enough! He certainly did not fear him enough to obey him! However, Jonah properly identified God—his God—as the "God of heaven who made the sea and the dry land." He identified him as the Creator and the one who had sent the storm.

Jonah also told them something else that we do not learn until we get to the end of verse 10. There we are told, "The men knew that he was fleeing from the presence of the Lord, because he had told them." In essence he said, "Yes, I fear the Lord, the maker of the sea and the dry land, the Lord of heaven, but I am running from him. I am disobeying him, and that is why we are having this horrible storm that is about to take your lives."

The reaction of the sailors is telling: they became "extremely frightened" (v. 10). Literally, it says, they "feared a great fear." They were afraid before, but now they were doubly afraid. Now they not only feared the sea but also the one who controls the sea. Amazingly, these sailors demonstrated a sensitivity and respect—yes fear—for God that Jonah did not. Jonah said, "I fear the Lord," but he was not praying; he was disobeying. He was not concerned. These sailors, on the other hand, were in real fear—fear of the one who controls the sea and the storm. They said to Jonah, "How could you do this?" This is probably more an exclamation than a question.[8] They wondered how *anybody* could do this. Jonah identified his God as the creator of all things. That was something the sailors' gods did not claim. It was inconceivable to them that Jonah was fleeing from the Creator.

6. Elizabeth Achtemeier (*Minor Prophets I.* New International Biblical Commentary [Peabody, MA: Hendrickson., 1996], 265) aptly notes, "They are not interested in Jonah's biography. They want to know what god he serves, for it is that god who is punishing Jonah by means of the storm. To the sailors' way of thinking, every god or goddess is attached to a particular location or people, and the sailors desperately need to identify the deity, in order to take measures to appease him or her."

7. H. L. Ellison, "Jonah" in *Expositor's Bible Commentary*, ed. Frank E. Gaebelein, Vol. 7 (Grand Rapids: Zondervan, 1985), 371.

8. Ellison, "Jonah," 372.

Jonah was humiliated in the eyes of those to whom he should have been a witness—Gentiles. There was a time in America and in other countries when even unbelievers held the church and Christians in high esteem. This was because of their integrity and commitment to truth and morality. For the most part Christians do not enjoy that elevated status anymore. Instead, Christians are the objects of ridicule. Yes, Jesus said that if we follow in his footsteps we will be persecuted, but the persecution we face is not always because of following him. Too often, the humiliation we suffer before the eyes of the world is because of collective and individual disobedience to God's will. Rather than transforming our world, the world has transformed us. Rather than our being in the world, the world is in us. Such behavior has results, and often it is humiliation before those to whom we should be a testimony.

Punishment

> So they said to him, "What should we do to you that the sea may become calm for us?"—for the sea was becoming increasingly stormy. He said to them, "Pick me up and throw me into the sea. Then the sea will become calm for you, for I know that on account of me this great storm has come upon you." However, the men rowed desperately to return to land but they could not, for the sea was becoming even stormier against them. Then they called on the Lord and said, "We earnestly pray, O Lord, do not let us perish on account of this man's life and do not put innocent blood on us; for You, O Lord, have done as You have pleased."
>
> So they picked up Jonah, threw him into the sea, and the sea stopped its raging. (Jonah 1:11–15)

Jonah also suffered punishment, or discipline, from God. The storm was not letting up; it was getting worse. So the sailors said, "What should we do to you that the sea may become calm for us?" These men were extremely anxious to know what they could do about this storm, now that they knew the cause of it, and they asked Jonah. It was Jonah's God who had brought the storm, and they naturally assumed Jonah would know his God best. Jonah said, "Throw me into the sea."

Jonah was right. He was right, in that, if he were cast into the sea, the storm would cease. But this was not repentance. Jonah at this point was not repenting. There was another answer he could have given—a repentant answer. That answer would have been, "I am ready to go to Nineveh.

Take me in that direction." I believe if he had said that and meant it, the storm would have ceased right then. Jonah, however, would rather die than repent. Is it not astonishing that Jonah would rather die in the sea than repent and do as God told him? Yet this is not a unique attitude. There are a couple of places in the New Testament where God tells us that the obstinate refusal of a believer to repent can lead to physical death (1 Cor. 11:27–30, where "sleep" is a euphemism for death; 1 John 5:16). It *can* lead to death; it certainly will bring discipline and sometimes very severe discipline. So it was for Jonah.

We get the impression that the sailors on this ship had quite a bit of character in spite of their pagan beliefs. They were reluctant to do what Jonah told them to do. Instead, they "rowed desperately" in an attempt to reach land, but the storm was growing worse and made their efforts useless. They finally concluded that they did not have any other choice but to cast Jonah overboard as he said. Still, they were reluctant to do it, and they prayed. The sailors "called on the Lord and said, 'We earnestly pray, O Lord, do not let us perish on account of this man's life and do not put innocent blood on us.'" Notice that now it was not their gods, they addressed, but the Lord (Yahweh), the true God. Their plea to God was that he not hold them responsible for Jonah's death. They could see no other choice, but they did not want to be held guilty for his death.

The sailors then recognized something that Jonah himself had not yet acknowledged—that God is sovereign. They said at the end of verse 14, "For You, O Lord, have done as You have pleased." The true God *is* sovereign. He does as he pleases, and no one can stand in his way. With that, they picked up Jonah and threw him into the sea, and the storm came to an end. This supernatural, miraculous storm God had brought upon them just as miraculously and instantly ceased when Jonah was cast into the sea.

At this point in the story, it would seem that Jonah had wasted his life by his own choice. As he sank into the sea, his life would appear to be over. He was like so many Christians we have known who have put their own desires ahead of loyalty to God and brought great, great trouble upon themselves as a result. In Jonah's case, his life seemed to have been wasted—so much so, that only the grace of God could save his life, and only the grace of God could salvage anything from it.

We serve a great God, however. Incredibly, even at this point, God had more plans for Jonah. Not only that, but he also had more plans for the sailors still in the boat.

Jonah's disobedience had obvious negative results for himself, as well as for those on the boat. It also had results for God as we see in verse 16.

RESULTS FOR GOD

Then the men feared the Lord greatly, and they offered a sacrifice to the Lord and made vows. (Jonah 1:16)

This is a truly remarkable verse. It is not at all what we might have expected. What might we have expected? Jonah had disobeyed God, ruined his life, and brought trouble upon himself and upon others. From all appearances it would seem he had ruined God's plans as well and brought disrespect upon the Lord. But we find something quite different in verse 16. Rather than dismissing Jonah's God, the sailors "feared the Lord greatly." Indeed, they "offered a sacrifice to the Lord and made vows." The sailors now feared the Lord and worshiped him by offering a sacrifice and making vows to him. What does all this mean? Some would argue that they were truly converted to faith in God. That may be saying too much, but we can say this: they now clearly had respect for the true God. They recognized and honored him. Whether they were true believers or not, we do not know, but they at least had taken a step in that direction.[9] Who knows what God might have done beyond that?

It is amazing that even through Jonah's disobedience God was exalted. It is amazing, but we see occurrences time and time again in the scriptural record of God using sinful people and even sinful actions to accomplish his purposes. Joseph told his wicked brothers who had sold him into slavery, "You meant evil against me, but God meant it for good" (Gen. 50:20). God used the pagan Persian king Cyrus to restore his people to their homeland and in Isaiah 45 speaks of Cyrus almost in messianic terms (vv. 1–6). God likewise used even Pilate and Herod to accomplish his goals and bring honor to himself. Even through Jonah's disobedience, unbelievers, Gentiles no less, were confronted with the truth. It is here we

---

9. Paul R. Fink ("Jonah" in *Liberty Bible Commentary*, ed. Jerry Falwell, Edward Hindson, and Woodrow Kroll [Nashville: Nelson, 1982], 1726) suggests, "These heathen sailors came to a true knowledge of Jehovah as their God." H. L. Ellison ("Jonah," 372), on the other hand, says, "Certainly there was a new respect for the God of Israel, a new understanding of his power; but there is no suggestion that these Phoenician sailors renounced their ancestral religion or made any efforts to discover what, apart from power, distinguished Yahweh from Baal or Ashtoreth."

really see the sovereign working of God. God had called Jonah to go to Gentiles in Assyria; instead, Jonah had run in the opposite direction in disobedience to God. Yet God still reached Gentiles with the truth in spite of Jonah's disobedience and even *through* his obstinate behavior.

Here is what we need to learn. God is sovereign. He will accomplish His purposes with or without our obedience. He does not need us, and He does not need our obedience, but He wants us, and he wants our obedience. He wants our loving obedience to his commands for our own good, for the good of those we have contact with in our lives, and for his own pleasure. It is wonderful reassurance that we cannot spoil God's plans no matter what we do. We cannot ruin his plans, but we can be a part of them. That is the amazing thing. He invites us to be a part of his plan—to fulfill the very purpose of our existence, to know the full blessing of God in our lives. No, we cannot ruin his plans, but we *can* ruin our lives by going our own way. The Lord wants us to be a part of his plan by obeying, serving, worshiping, and glorifying him.

PERSONAL APPLICATION

- Can you think of an example of how your sins have affected others?
- Are you sometimes reluctant to confess sins God already knows about? Why? Think of two things you can do to counter this tendency.
- Is there evidence in your life that you fear God? Do you fear him enough? How do you know?
- How can you reclaim respect for your faith in a world where faith is often ridiculed?

FOR FURTHER STUDY

- Read the article "Ships and Boats" in the *New Bible Dictionary* (Eerdmans) or a similar article in another Bible reference work.
- Read the following passages related to God's discipline of believers and develop an outline of the biblical teaching: 1 Corinthians 11:27–34; Hebrews 12:1–13; 1 John 5:16.
- Use a concordance to find verses that speak of the fear of God. Write a definition of the fear of the Lord based on these verses. Compare your definition to others you can find in commentaries or other references.

8

A Prophet's Prayer

Jonah 1:17–2:10

HISTORY PROVES THAT WE human beings are rather short-sighted—so short-sighted, in fact, that some of the most significant events in history went largely unnoticed at the time they occurred. One of the most important events of the twentieth century occurred at Kitty Hawk, North Carolina on December 17, 1903. The Wright brothers made their famous flight on that day. The next day, that event, the first powered flight of a heavier-than-air craft carrying a human being, was reported in only three newspapers. Twenty-one newspapers had been informed of the flight, but only three reported it. The Associated Press had the story and could have distributed it to hundreds of papers but chose instead to ignore it.[1]

When we think of Jonah and the book of Jonah, we immediately think of the fish that swallowed the wayward prophet. We remember that Jonah remained in the fish for three days and then was discharged. That is what everybody remembers, but as we read this passage and look at this amazing event, it seems that the really significant event was not so much this miracle—and a spectacular miracle it was—but what happened *inside* the fish. One verse at the end of chapter 1 tells us in very plain, easy-to-understand language that Jonah was swallowed by a fish. One verse at the end of chapter 2 says that the fish spit him out. There is no detailed description—only these few words. But between these two verses is Jonah's prayer, and that was the most significant matter in this whole miraculous incident. In a sense, the miracle of the fish simply provided the context for Jonah's prayer.

1. Charles Ludwig, *The Wright Brothers: They Gave Us Wings* (Milford, MI.: Mott Media, 1985), 146.

THE CONTEXT OF JONAH'S PRAYER

And the Lord appointed a great fish to swallow Jonah, and Jonah
was in the stomach of the fish three days and three nights. (1:17)

God had made it clear that he would not allow Jonah to continue in his
rebellion against God and his plan. The Lord had brought the storm upon
the sea, which eventually led to Jonah's being cast overboard. But the Lord
was not yet finished with the Israelite prophet.

We are told that "the Lord appointed a great fish to swallow Jonah."
This is a very clear, straightforward statement. Oh, but we lack imagina-
tion! This verse is one of the most ridiculed in the entire Bible by those
who reject the authority and inerrancy of Scripture. It is depressing in a
sense, but it is also laughable to read what some people have made out of
this verse in an attempt to rid the story of the supernatural. Perhaps the
most absurd suggestion is that this verse really means that Jonah recov-
ered from his ordeal in the sea by spending three days at an inn called
"The Fish."[2] In other words, he really was not swallowed by a fish; rather
he spent three days at the Fish Motel. It is truly amazing the lengths to
which people will go to make the Bible conform to their own precon-
ceived and sin-conceived ideas. It is far better to simply believe what God
says rather than what some people say about what God says. And what
God says here could be no clearer.

The text says that God "appointed" a fish. This does not mean he
created a fish especially for this event. Rather it means he chose, or determined that, this particular fish was going to carry out this particular
assignment.[3] What kind of fish was it? It was a big one. That is about all
we know for sure. The King James Version uses the word "whale" in the
New Testament when Jesus speaks of this event (Matt. 12:40), but that is
not the best translation. The Greek word simply means sea creature or sea
monster.[4] Even though a whale is not a *fish* as we know it today, the word

---

2. This is cited by David J. Clark, Norm Mundhenk, Eugene A. Nida, and Brynmor F.
Price in *A Handbook on the Books of Obadiah, Jonah, and Micah* (New York: United Bible
Societies, 1993), 73.

3. C. F. Keil and Franz Delitzsch, *Commentary on the Old Testament*, Vol. 10 (reprint,
Grand Rapids: Eerdmans, 1977), 398.

4. See Walter Bauer, William F Arndt, and F. Wilbur Gingrich, *A Greek-English
Lexicon of the New Testament and Other Early Christian Literature* (Chicago: University
of Chicago Press, 1957), 432; and W. E. Vine, Merrill F. Unger, and William White Jr.,
Vine's Complete Expository Dictionary of Old and New Testament Words (Nashville:

used in Matthew 12:40 could be used of a whale. Whales, however, are relatively rare in the Mediterranean.[5]

We do not know what kind of fish this was, but we know that fish exist that could do this. Fish have been caught that were subsequently found to have swallowed other fish weighing up to 1500 pounds. There is even an oft-cited incident from 1891 of a man on a whaling ship who, in the process of attempting to harpoon a whale, fell overboard and was lost. Later when the whale was killed and opened up, it is reported that the man was found alive inside the whale. We should be careful, however, about citing this or similar stories without thorough documentation. Although this is a very popular story, there is some question as to its accuracy.[6] The fact is that we do not need illustrations or examples. This was a miracle! And by definition a miracle is an extremely rare thing. Probably the most miraculous aspect of this is not that the fish swallowed Jonah but that the fish was there at the right place at the right time to do the very thing God wanted it to do.

Jonah 2:1 might lead us to believe that Jonah did not pray at all until the end of this three-day period in the fish. He did pray at the end of that period, but that was not the first time he prayed. Verse 2, as we will see, looks back to some prior time when he prayed, shortly after he was thrown into the sea. The essence of his prayer then was, "Help!" As he sank into the sea, he cried out for help. The Lord's answer to that prayer was a big fish. The fish was not God's means of punishment; the fish was God's means of saving Jonah from drowning. Granted, Jonah probably was not convinced at the time that this was his deliverance. To him it probably was simply a matter of which was the worst way to go—death by drowning or death by digestion.

Jonah was in the stomach of the fish for three days and three nights. Why three days and three nights? Maybe it just took that long for the fish to get back to the coast of Palestine to discharge his passenger. Apparently God wanted this experience to continue for some period of time in order to give Jonah time enough to contemplate what God was doing. After all, Jonah did not pray this prayer in chapter 2 until after three days and

---

Nelson, 1984), 672.

5. Keil and Delitzsch, *Commentary on the Old Testament*, 10:398.

6. Desmond Alexander, "Jonah" in David W. Baker, T. Desmond Alexander, and Bruce K. Waltke, *Obadiah, Jonah and Micah* (Downer's Grove, IL: InterVarsity, 1988), 111.

three nights. The Lord was giving him time to realize that this really was deliverance, not punishment. He was giving Jonah time to repent.

There is another reason, and it is found in a well-known passage in chapter 12 of Matthew. In verses 39–40 Jesus rebuked some scribes and Pharisees, telling them, "An evil and adulterous generation craves for a sign; and yet no sign shall be given to it but the sign of Jonah the prophet; for just as Jonah was three days and three nights in the belly of the sea monster, so will the Son of Man be three days and three nights in the heart of the earth." The fact that Jonah was in the belly of the fish for that length of time was an illustration or foreshadowing of what Jesus would go through when he died. He would be three days and three nights in the tomb.

Now at this point, we could skip from Jonah 1:17 to 2:10 and not miss anything in the narrative. But we would miss what is in many ways the key to the whole book of Jonah, and that is Jonah's prayer. Instead of details about this unique experience of being swallowed alive and preserved alive, we are given a psalm of thanksgiving, a prayer that focuses upon God and highlights his divine character.

THE CONTENT OF JONAH'S PRAYER

We should first note a couple of points about the nature of this prayer. First, it was spoken while Jonah was in the belly of the fish. He recalled this prayer later on and recorded it in this book, but it was prayed while he was in the fish. Second, there is in this prayer no petition or cry for deliverance. Jonah does not ask God for anything. This is a prayer of thanksgiving for deliverance from drowning. It is a prayer of commitment and a prayer of repentance. Third, the language Jonah used comes directly from the Psalms. While there are no extended quotations from Psalms, there are expressions and phrases that come directly from the Psalms.[7] That tells us something. It tells us that as disobedient, as stubborn, and as belligerent as Jonah was, somewhere along the line he had absorbed the Word of God, and when he turned to God in prayer at this time, the very words of Scripture come from his mouth. This prayer is very poetic. It is not something one would come up with out of nowhere. Jonah had so absorbed the Psalms that the very expressions of the psalmists naturally flow from his mouth.

7. See H. L. Ellison, "Jonah" in *Expositor's Bible Commentary*, ed. Frank E. Gaebelein, Vol. 7 (Grand Rapids: Zondervan, 1985), 364.

Thanksgiving

> Then Jonah prayed to the Lord his God from the stomach of the fish, and he said, "I called out of my distress to the Lord, And He answered me. I cried for help from the depth of Sheol; You heard my voice. For You had cast me into the deep, Into the heart of the seas, And the current engulfed me. All Your breakers and billows passed over me. So I said, 'I have been expelled from Your sight. Nevertheless I will look again toward Your holy temple.' "Water encompassed me to the point of death. The great deep engulfed me, Weeds were wrapped around my head. I descended to the roots of the mountains. The earth with its bars was around me forever, But You have brought up my life from the pit, O Lord my God." (Jonah 2:1–6)

Jonah's prayer, spoken while still in the fish's stomach, was first and foremost a prayer of thanksgiving. He is near the end of this three-day period in the fish now, but he is looking back to when he was first thrown into the sea. Jonah recalls that at that time he had cried out to the Lord in his distress, and the Lord had responded to his plea. How had the Lord answered Jonah's cry for help? As we said, the fish was God's answer, for it was God's means of saving Jonah from drowning. God, in fact, was answering the prayer even before Jonah spoke the words. For some reason, as he sank hopelessly into the sea to drown there, something clicked in Jonah's mind, and he cried out to God for help, and God's answer was there waiting.

Jonah cried in distress and from "the depth of Sheol." Interestingly, the word translated "depth" is literally the word for belly, or womb.[8] Jonah was about to go into the belly of the fish, but at this point he was in the belly of sheol. *Sheol* is a Hebrew word for the place of the dead, or the grave.[9] The NIV translates it "grave." So Jonah was saying he was in the very depths of the grave.

Again, in Matthew 12:40 Jesus said, "Just as Jonah was three days and three nights in the belly of the sea monster, so will the Son of Man be three days and three nights in the heart of the earth." Here Jonah was saying, "I was in the depths of sheol, or the grave." Did Jonah actually die? There are some who say yes, that Jonah actually died in the belly of the fish and was

---

8. Alexander, "Jonah," 113

9. William A. Van Gemeren, "Sheol" in *Evangelical Dictionary of Theology*, 2d ed., ed. Walter A. Elwell (Grand Rapids: Baker Academic, 2001), 1098–99; R. Laird Harris, "Sheol," *TWOT*, 2:892–93.

resurrected to life, thus becoming the perfect pattern for what Jesus experienced many years later. I do not believe that is what happened. Jonah was using poetic language from the Psalms here (cf. Pss. 18:5; 30:3; 88:3; 116:3). As such he also was using a common device employed by David and others: hyperbole. We often call it exaggeration. Jonah was expressing in the strongest terms he could his grave condition. He was saying that he was as good as dead. Indeed he was as good as dead when he cried out to God. He had been thrown into the middle of the Mediterranean Sea, where there was no hope for survival.

Verses 3–6 elaborate in very poetic language on Jonah's condition in the sea. He says, "For You had cast me into the deep, into the heart of the seas." But who was it that had cast Jonah into the sea? Was it not the sailors who had reluctantly thrown him overboard? But Jonah now says, "You—God—cast me into the deep." We see here that Jonah was beginning to get the hint, for he recognized, finally, that God ultimately was the one who had brought this about. Yes, the sailors were the ones who physically had thrown him into the sea, but God was the one who had arranged it all. He was the one who was sovereignly controlling the weather, the sailors, the fish—everything. Jonah thus is recognizing that God is sovereign in all this. He was the one who ultimately cast him "into the deep."

If we read through the description in these verses carefully, we can almost feel Jonah sinking deeper and deeper and deeper into the sea. He says, "The current engulfed me." The idea here is that he was caught in the current. He was at the mercy of the sea. As he sank helplessly into the deep, he looked up and saw the waves, "the breakers and billows," passing over top.

Then in verse 4 Jonah says, "So I said, 'I have been expelled from Your sight.'" At that point, as Jonah sank into the sea, with no hope of survival, the thought struck him that now he had been expelled, he had been banished from the sight of God. Remember that Jonah was running from the presence of the Lord. Fleeing from God's presence was what he was trying to do in the first place, but he found he could not do it. But as he sank to his death, he had the terrifying thought that he actually had got what he wanted—that he had actually been banished from the sight of God. It must have been a horrible thought, for is that not what hell is—banishment from God's presence? Yes, hell is punishment, but much of that punishment is that one is forever separated from God. Jonah was trying to separate himself from the presence of God, but it was only when God threw him into the sea that he really felt the full impact of what that meant.

But look at the contrast. "Nevertheless I will look again toward Your holy temple." Jonah looks back and says, "Yes, at that moment, I felt I had been banished from the sight of God, but now I can say, I will once again look toward the temple."[10] The idea of looking toward the temple might seem a strange expression to us, but it was an expression of faith. Jonah actually may never have even seen the temple, for the temple was in Jerusalem, and Jonah lived in the northern kingdom of Israel. The way a godly Israelite demonstrated faith in God was by worshiping in the temple. If he could not be in that unique place where God's presence was manifested in Old Testament times, he would face toward the temple. We see this in Daniel 6:10. Daniel was exiled to Babylon, yet three times a day, he faced toward Jerusalem and prayed. So Jonah essentially was saying, "What a contrast. I felt like I was completely banished from God's presence, but now I will once again worship him; I will look toward his holy temple."

Verse 5 continues the description of Jonah's sinking down into the sea. He says, "Water encompassed me to the point of death,[11] the great deep engulfed me, weeds were wrapped around my head." This whole description conveys the idea of complete helplessness. He is surrounded by the weeds and entombed in the water. He is utterly helpless. He sinks deeper and deeper—so deep, in fact, that in verse 6 he says, "I descended to the roots of the mountains," that is, to the foundations of the mountains. He went to the very bottom. There, he says, "The earth with its bars was around me forever." What does this mean? Again, Jonah is using poetic language. He describes his situation as being like the bars of a prison closing shut on him. The prison bars of death were closing, shutting him in. There was no escape, yet he goes on to say, "You have brought up my life from the pit." The "pit" here is probably a synonym for sheol, the grave. Thus as he sinks to the very bottom of the sea, Jonah describes his im-

10. Some translate the phrase as a question: "How will I look again?" (cf. NRSV; NJB). The NASB is probably correct however, in expressing a determination to pray in spite of Jonah's apparent banishment (Ellison, "Jonah," 377).

11. Most versions opt for a translation that conveys the idea of imminent death. The old NASB, like the KJV, translated more literally, "encompassed me to the very soul." "Soul" is the usual translation of the Hebrew *nephesh*, but the word has a wide range of meanings (cf. *BDB*, 659–61; Bruce K. Waltke, "*Nephesh*," *TWOT*, 2:587–91). Some argue that "throat" is the best translation here, as reflected in NJB's "neck."

minent death as an imprisonment offering him no escape, no way out. It was only "when Jonah gave up hope of surviving and could sink no lower, God intervened and saved him" and brought up his life from the pit.[12]

As noted, this portion of the prayer consists of thanksgiving. What was it that Jonah was thanking God for? First, he was thanking him for deliverance from drowning. Second, he was thanking God for a renewed opportunity to worship. Perhaps none of us has been as close to death as Jonah was—at a point where there was no hope and only God could save us. But every day we live is by God's grace. Every day we have is as much a testimony to the grace of God as Jonah's deliverance from the sea. Every day we have is a day God has given to us for a purpose—to worship him, to serve him, to honor him. That is our reason for existence, and it is something we should certainly be thankful for.

Repentance

"While I was fainting away, I remembered the Lord; And my prayer came to You, Into Your holy temple." (Jonah 2:7)

In verse 7 we finally start to see Jonah's repentance. While he was "fainting away," or dying, he *remembered* the Lord. Does that mean he had completely forgotten about God? No. This same word is used in a number of interesting contexts in the Old Testament. For example, in the midst of the flood, as Noah and his family and the animals were in the ark, Scripture tells us, "The Lord remembered Noah" (Gen. 8:1). Noah had not slipped God's mind. This word does not just convey the idea of mental activity; it speaks of an active work. When God remembered Noah, it meant that he was turning his thoughts toward Noah to bring about the completion of this work. Remembering is a determination to do something; it is not just mentally recalling to mind.[13] When Jonah said, "I remembered the Lord," his thoughts at this point turned to the Lord in the sense that now he was going to do what God wanted him to do.

Note that the phrase "I remembered the Lord" here is parallel to "my prayer came to You." They are synonymous expressions as indicated by the device of parallelism so often used in Hebrew poetry. In fact, some Bible

12. Lloyd J. Olgilvie, *Hosea, Joel, Amos, Obadiah, Jonah.* The Communicator's Commentary (Waco: Word, 1991), 415.

13. Andrew Bowling, *"zakar,"* *TWOT,* 1:241.

versions, translate this word "prayed" rather than "remembered."[14] Jonah's remembering the Lord was a determination to do something, but it was also a prayer. His prayer came into God's "holy temple." Here, he is talking not about the temple in Jerusalem as he was in verse 4 but about God's temple in heaven.

Was this real repentance? Yes, it was, but repentance is always demonstrated by commitment. Repentance, like "remembering," is not just a mental activity either. It is a commitment; it is turning around. So it is we see in the next two verses Jonah's repentance borne out in his commitment.

Commitment

> Those who regard vain idols Forsake their faithfulness, But I will sacrifice to You With the voice of thanksgiving. That which I have vowed I will pay. Salvation is from the Lord. (Jonah 2:8–9)

Verse 8 says, "Those who regard vain idols forsake their faithfulness," but what does this mean? It is not entirely clear what it means. In fact, this verse is extremely difficult to translate.[15] The idea conveyed by the NASB seems to be that those who cling to idols are eventually going to abandon them for other gods or something else, because they are going to find that their idols are worthless. The NIV says, "Those who cling to worthless idols forfeit the grace that could be theirs." In other words, as long as they are clinging to these idols, they are turning their backs on the grace of God. No matter how we translate this, however, we can say this: Jonah is making a contrast between clinging to vain, false idols and clinging to the Lord. We see the contrast in verse 9: "But I will sacrifice to You with the voice of thanksgiving. That which I have vowed, I will pay."

What may have been in Jonah's mind were the sailors on the boat. They prayed to their gods—worthless idols—when the storm engulfed them. They did not see any other hope. And what good did their prayers do? They did them no good. They were talking to gods that do not exist. Their efforts were vain, worthless. Is it not interesting that those sailors, who showed more character than Jonah did, were praying to their idols? But Jonah said, "I will sacrifice to You." It is almost as if he were saying, "All

---

14. cf. *Today's English Version*.
15. Alexander, "Jonah," 117

their prayers were to no avail, but, as disobedient as I have been, I can still call on the Lord at the last moment and know that he is faithful and will hear." This was a tremendous expression of faith on Jonah's part, especially when we consider where he had come from.

In verse 9, Jonah promises to offer sacrifice. In the Old Testament, sacrifice was a means of worshiping God, but it was also a way of confessing one's sin to God. Jonah thus promises to worship God and perhaps confess his sin. He also promises to fulfill a vow. What was Jonah's vow? The text does not say, so we are left to guess. My guess is that it was a vow to go to Nineveh. Finally, he had said, "OK, I am ready to go." We see no argument from Jonah. We see only submission. His repentance is demonstrated by his commitment to worship God again, to confess his sin, and to fulfill his vow, to do what he has promised to do.

Jonah concludes his prayer with this: "Salvation is from the Lord." This pretty much summarizes all that the Lord had done for him. Both in the boat and in the sea, it was the Lord who had delivered. He had proved himself as the only God who could answer, the only God who could save. Interestingly enough, Jonah would soon see God deliver even the wicked population of Nineveh.

That is Jonah's prayer. As we look at it again, notice that there were no requests, no petitions, only thanksgiving, commitment, and repentance. This points out an interesting fact. It seems many characters in the Bible understood something we seem to have largely forgotten. Yes, prayer is asking God for things for us and for others, but that is not all prayer is. Prayer is not just about us and other people. It is about God. Let me suggest a little exercise, and let me warn you that it is difficult. Try praying for ten minutes without asking God for anything. If you attempt that, it is going to focus your mind on an important aspect of prayer that we sometimes skip over. Often our prayers can be described like this: Thank you, God, for this and that; now let's get to the important stuff—what I need, what my family needs, what others need. I am convinced our prayers need to be more God-focused, more directed toward thanksgiving, adoration, and commitment to God.

THE RESULT OF JONAH'S PRAYER

Then the Lord commanded the fish, and it vomited Jonah up onto the dry land. (Jonah 2:10)

This verse describes what apparently was the result of Jonah's prayer. As we said before, Jonah is not really the main character in this book. God is the main character, and he is seen in what he does. The Lord commanded the fish. The Lord was the one in control of the fish, just as he had been in control of everything else that had happened to Jonah. The fish responded to the Lord's command by transporting Jonah, apparently back to the coast, presumably of the Holy Land, Israel, where he vomited him up onto the dry land.

If the Lord has a job for us and we are willing to do it, God is going to take care of all the details. He will get us to the place he wants us to be. It probably will not be as dramatic as it was with Jonah, but he will get us to where we need to be. He wants people who are willing, people who are submissive to his will.

There are several things we should learn from this passage. First, God is faithful even when we are not (cf. 2 Tim. 2:13). There is probably no better example of someone who was unfaithful than Jonah. This was a prophet of God, a man to whom the Lord directly spoke, but he rebelled against the Lord's command. Yet God pursued him. God did not give up on him but went to great lengths to secure Jonah's repentance and obedience. Thus, a second lesson here is that God wants very, very much for us to obey him—for our own good but also for his glory. God does not need us or our obedience. He can accomplish his goals without us, but he wants us. And he wants our obedience, and he will lovingly, and sometimes sternly, seek to secure it.

Finally, of course, God forgives. No matter what we have done, no matter how far we have gone, no matter how many times we have turned from him, he is still more than willing to forgive us. And not only is he willing to forgive us, but he still has plans for us, and he can still use us. That is what Jonah teaches us.

PERSONAL APPLICATION

- Does Scripture come readily to your mind when you encounter trials? If not, how can you develop this habit?

- Are you as committed to prayer as you should be? How does the time you give to prayer compare with that of some adherents of other religions? By what standard should you measure your commitment?

- How much of your prayers are given to thanksgiving? Try the exercise mentioned near the end of the chapter—praying for ten minutes without asking God for anything. After doing this exercise, take a sheet of paper and list fifty things you can thank God for.

- Take some time to recall ways in which God has shown his faithfulness to you. Share these with family or fellow believers the first time you have an opportunity.

For Further Study

- Go to a church library, or even a public library, and find several different ways authors have explained Jonah's being swallowed by the fish. What is the problem with trying to explain miracles?

- "A recognition that God is behind every event in our lives—whether good or bad—is a sign of spiritual growth and maturity." Evaluate this statement from Scripture. Note especially statements such as those in Jonah 2:3 and Genesis 45:7–8.

- Theologian Henry C. Thiessen *(Lectures in Systematic Theology)* noted that repentance has an *intellectual* element (a change of view with regard to sin, God, and self), an *emotional* element (sorrow for sin), and a *volitional* element (a turning away from sin). Do you see these three elements in Jonah's prayer? Why is it important that these three elements of repentance be clearly taught? What are the potential hazards if one or more of these elements are ignored?

9

A Great Awakening

Jonah 3

IN ISAIAH 55:9, GOD says this: "My ways [are] higher than your ways."
This is nowhere clearer than in some of the great revivals or spiritual
awakenings in history. God does not always work the way we might expect
him to. In the seventh century B.C. in the nation of Judah, God chose to
bring about a great revival, but he did not choose the oldest and the wisest;
he did not even choose one of his own prophets. He chose a twenty-year-
old king, the son of a very wicked ruler and the grandson of perhaps the
most wicked ruler in Judah's history. That young king's name was Josiah
(2 Kings 22–23; 2 Chron. 34–35). In America in the early 1700s, God
brought about what has come to be known as the Great Awakening—a
great spiritual movement that engulfed the colonies. One of the primary
instruments of the Great Awakening was a squeaky voiced, nearsighted
preacher who each Sunday took his sermon manuscript, held it in front of
his face, and read it to his congregation. His name was Jonathan Edwards.
God does not always use the methods we might expect him to. He does
not always use the people we might expect him to.

American Christians probably would all agree that what the United
States needs more than anything else today, indeed what our world needs
more than anything else, is a great spiritual awakening, a great turning
to God. Certainly we should be praying for that. If God chooses to answer that prayer, however, he might very well surprise us. Who knows?
He might even find a selfish, bigoted, wayward believer and *force* him to
preach God's message of repentance. If that sounds a bit far-fetched, it

should not. That is essentially what God did with Jonah, and the result was a great awakening in Nineveh. Jonah was selfish, he was bigoted, and he was disobedient. And God pretty much had to force him to go to Nineveh and preach his message. Jonah did go, however, and amazingly enough God used this man to bring about one of the great spiritual awakenings in history. Jonah is not our pattern as we think about our task in the world. He does provide us with some important lessons, but he is not a very good example, in spite of the fact that God used him. The great awakening under Jonah, however, illustrates some of the necessary ingredients in any spiritual awakening, and we will look at chapter 3 of Jonah in that light.

JONAH'S OBEDIENCE

> Now the word of the Lord came to Jonah the second time, saying, "Arise, go to Nineveh the great city and proclaim to it the proclamation which I am going to tell you." So Jonah arose and went to Nineveh according to the word of the Lord. Now Nineveh was an exceedingly great city, a three days' walk. Then Jonah began to go through the city one day's walk; and he cried out and said, "Yet forty days and Nineveh will be overthrown." (Jonah 3:1–4)

Wherever we see spiritual awakening on a mass scale, it is always accompanied by the obedience of God's people. In verses 1–4, we see the obedience of Jonah. It did not come easily, of course. This was the second time God had called Jonah to do this. If we look back at the first few verses of chapter 1, we see there almost identical language. The problem really was not the Ninevites; the problem was Jonah. The Ninevites were wicked, evil people, but they were just doing what came naturally. The problem was Jonah. He was not doing what should have come naturally to a believer. We think the problem in the world today is the wicked people, the evil that seems to be permeating our society. The problem is not the wicked people; they are just doing what wicked people do. The problem is the church—believers.

So often there is very, very little difference between Christians and the world when it comes to motivations, aspirations, and sadly, even ethics. The problem is not the world; the problem is our failure to fully obey God. So it was with Jonah.

Jonah was given a rather simple task in some respects. God told him to go to Nineveh and proclaim exactly what God told him. Jonah did not have to be creative. He did not have to be a marketing genius. He did not even have to come up with a sermon. He simply had to repeat what God was going to tell him. This time Jonah obeyed. Before, he had run. He had disobeyed God, and God had had to do a very dramatic work in his life. But now he obeyed. He "arose and went to Nineveh according to the word of the Lord."

Jonah's mission was simply to repeat God's message. That did not mean it was not a hazardous mission, however. Imagine an Israelite walking through the streets of Nineveh, Assyria's largest city, proclaiming that the God of Israel was going to bring judgment on this land? Let us put this in modern terms. The ancient city of Nineveh was in Assyria. That land is now within the modern nation of Iraq. Now, imagine a Jew today, from Israel, being told to go to Iraq, march into Baghdad, and start preaching that judgment is coming unless the people repent and turn to Israel's God. That gives a pretty good idea of what Jonah's mission was, and maybe an idea of why he was more than a little hesitant to carry it out. It was a simple message but a hazardous mission.

We are told that Nineveh was a "great city, a three day's walk." This could mean that it took three days to walk around the city. Or it could mean that it took three days to walk through the city, either winding one's way through it or traveling straight across it. The problem with that is that modern archaeologists have unearthed the ancient city of Nineveh and have found that the walled city was no more than a mile across at its widest point. It could not hold the kind of population that is spoken of in the next chapter, and it certainly would not take three days to walk around it or through it. So how do we explain this? We see again in Jonah 3:2 (cf. 1:2), that Nineveh is described as a "great city." This expression simply means "Greater Nineveh." It includes the walled city and the area surrounding it. In fact, today we know that this was a four-city complex, with Nineveh being the largest of the four. It could hold well over 100,000 people.[1] So we are not talking simply about the city proper but about Greater Nineveh. Thus, the description of a three-day's walk makes sense. Probably what is meant is that it took Jonah three days to walk up and down the streets of this great metropolitan area, declaring this message.

Verse 3 also describes Nineveh as "an exceedingly great city." Literally, this can be translated "a great city to God." In other words, it was a city that

---

1. Desmond Alexander, "Jonah" in David W. Baker, T. Desmond Alexander, and Bruce K. Waltke, *Obadiah, Jonah and Micah* (Downer's Grove, IL: InterVarsity, 1988), 55–59.

was important to God.[2] Not only was it an important city in terms of the empire of Assyria, but it also was a city that was important to God. And that is really why God sent Jonah there. It was important that these people hear the message God had for them. God was concerned about them, even if Jonah was not.

Jonah thus began his walk through this great city, and he began to cry out, "Yet forty days and Nineveh will be overthrown." The message was a message of judgment. In fact, "overthrown" (*hapak*) is the same Hebrew word that is used in Genesis for the destruction of Sodom and Gomorrah (Gen. 19:21, 25, 29). He was warning of a catastrophic destruction that was coming upon this city. We have to understand, however, that this is not the entire sermon of Jonah. It is a summary of Jonah's message. We ascertain from these few words that Jonah's announcement was a message of judgment, but clearly the Ninevites understood more than what this brief summary conveys. Clearly, there was more to the message than just this, as we will see later, and that should not surprise us. The Bible very seldom records a complete sermon. Rather, it gives us summaries (See e.g., Luke 24:25–27; Acts 2:40; 8:35; 28:23–28).

Jonah's basic message, however, was one of judgment coming in forty days. Why forty days? Why not tomorrow? Why not three days? The implication is that the Ninevites were given forty days to repent. They were given forty days' opportunity to repent before the judgment would come.

Jonah obeyed—finally. And that was key to what God was going to do. Indeed, we can expect no great work of God until we see God's people obeying him.

NINEVEH'S REPENTANCE

The People

> Then the people of Nineveh believed in God; and they called a fast and put on sackcloth from the greatest to the least of them. (Jonah 3:5)

The second element in any great revival, of course, is the repentance of people on a mass scale. In verses 5–9 we see Nineveh's repentance. It comes in two stages. First, we see the response of the people, and then we

---

2. Alexander, "Jonah," 119.

see the response of the king. Verse 5 says the people of Nineveh believed *in God*. The NIV says they believed *God*. Does this mean they simply believed the message of coming judgment? Well, they did believe that, but it means much more than that. Jonah used a particular word here that means more than simply believing what someone says. It expresses the idea of trusting in a person. They trusted not just the message but also the Person. They trusted God. This word is used to express certainty or assurance.[3] It means they were converted, and that is truly astounding. On top of that, it seems that Jonah had begun to walk through the city just one day's walk—he still had two days ahead of him—and there was this immediate response of the entire city! It is almost unbelievable.

How do we account for such a response? There could have been any number of factors that God used here, depending upon the exact date when Jonah appeared in Nineveh preaching God's message. If Jonah had showed up a little after 760 B.C., his arrival could have fit in like this.[4] In 765 B.C. Nineveh had experienced a great plague. Two years later they witnessed a total solar eclipse. And a few years later in 759, another plague struck the area. Then Jonah appeared announcing coming judgment. His appearance following these events, which the people of Nineveh might very well have interpreted as God's displeasure with them, would have been very striking to the inhabitants of the city.

There is another possibility suggested by the words of Jesus. Luke 11:29–30 says, "As the crowds were increasing, He (Jesus) began to say, 'This generation is a wicked generation; it seeks for a sign, and yet no sign will be given to it but the sign of Jonah. For just as Jonah became a sign to the Ninevites, so will the Son of Man be to this generation.'" Jonah "became a sign to the Ninevites." Jesus did not say Jonah brought a sign or presented a sign; he said Jonah himself *was* a sign to the Ninevites. Jesus did not explain exactly what that means; so we are left to speculate, and what we say here is speculation. Word of Jonah's unique experience may have reached Nineveh before him. If the people of Nineveh had heard about this unique occurrence of a man being swallowed by a fish, surviving for three days, and being spit back out on dry land, and then they saw him walking into their city, this might have had a profound effect upon those people. It is hard to know exactly what all went on in the belly of

3. Jack B. Scott, "aman," *TWOT*, 1:51.

4. See Gerald H. Twombly, *Major Themes from the Minor Prophets* (Winona Lake, IN: BMH Books, 1981), 67, and Alexander, "Jonah," 80.

the fish, but all the gastric juices for digestion may well have affected the appearance of Jonah. Whether it bleached out his skin, which seems likely, or caused him to have a grotesque appearance when he showed up in Nineveh, we do not know. It is possible that God might have used something like that to make Jonah a sign—a sign of something beyond himself, a sign that his message was true and would indeed be fulfilled.

That is speculation. The only certain answer we have as to why there was this mass repentance is that it was a miraculous work of God. After all, why does anybody repent? It is because God the Holy Spirit does a work inside a person—a work we cannot explain. It is a work of God, and that is the only way we can explain anything this incredible happening. "Nothing remotely approximating this has ever taken place in the history of revivals," Charles Feinberg wrote.[5] How many evangelists today have seen anything like this happen? How many have preached one message and seen 100,000 people suddenly repent? And repent they did. They believed in God and "called a fast and put on sackcloth from the greatest to the least of them." Fasting, of course, is a way of devoting oneself to prayer. The use of sackcloth was a way of expressing repentance.[6]

The King

> When the word reached the king of Nineveh, he arose from his throne, laid aside his robe from him, covered himself with sackcloth and sat on the ashes. He issued a proclamation and it said, "In Nineveh by the decree of the king and his nobles: Do not let man, beast, herd, or flock taste a thing. Do not let them eat or drink water. But both man and beast must be covered with sackcloth; and let men call on God earnestly that each may turn from his wicked way and from the violence which is in his hands. Who knows, God may turn and relent and withdraw His burning anger so that we will not perish." (Jonah 3:6–9)

"When the word reached the king of Nineveh," he responded much as the people had. What did he hear? Did he hear about the people's response, or did he hear about Jonah's message? Probably both. But the people and their reaction led the way. In this case, the nation's leader was the follower. This is a reminder of the influence people can have upon their leaders.

---

5. Charles L. Feinberg, *The Minor Prophets* (Chicago: Moody, 1990), 145.
6. See below on Jonah 3:6.

Even this pagan monarch took notice of his people's reaction to the foreign prophet. The king responded with repentance. He covered himself with sackcloth and sat on the ashes. What does this mean? We see these very actions a number of times in the Old Testament (cf. Neh. 9:1–2; Dan. 9:3–4). Sackcloth and ashes was a common means of expressing grief, humility, or repentance. The king was probably expressing all three ideas here: grief over the nation's sin, humility before God, and repentance. Sackcloth was a very coarse material usually made of goats' hair and used for making sacks. Shepherds often wore sackcloth because it was very durable and also very cheap.[7] It was not worn by the rich or middle class. It was not even worn by the poor normally. People donned sackcloth only on certain occasions to express these ideas—repentance, grief, or humility. Ashes were used metaphorically for that which is worthless or detestable.[8] These two symbolic acts together—putting on sackcloth and sitting in ashes—were used throughout the Middle East to express repentance and the grief and humility that accompanied it. Why did these acts come to symbolize repentance? It was probably because they were identified with humility and lowliness. This was not the kind of thing one did on a normal basis. It was "below" a person to wear such clothing, and it certainly was "below" a person to sit in the ashes unless some drastic situation called for it.

On this occasion, the king himself put on sackcloth and sat in the ashes. He also issued a proclamation, calling for the outward signs of repentance and submission to God on behalf of all the people. He wanted everyone to fast and pray and put on sackcloth, and he even extended his decree to the animals. This might seem like a very strange idea, but it is something we know was practiced by some peoples.[9] But what was the purpose of this practice? After all, an animal cannot repent or show grief or humility. Perhaps it was a recognition that man's actions affect the animal world. Certainly human sin has affected the animal kingdom, but in this case the practice probably reflected some superstition on the part of the people. Whatever the thinking behind this act, it does indicate how serious the king was. He wanted to cover all the bases. He wanted sincere repentance and prayer.

7. J. A. Thompson, "Sackcloth" in *The New Bible Dictionary*, ed. J. D. Douglas (Grand Rapids: Eerdmans, 1962), 1112.

8. P. A. Blair, "Ashes" in *The New Bible Dictionary*, 95; R. K. Harrison, "Ashes" in *The International Standard Bible Encyclopedia*, revised, ed. Geoffrey Bromiley (Grand Rapids: Eerdmans, 1979), 1:318.

9. C. F. Keil and Franz Delitzsch, *Commentary on the Old Testament*, Vol. 10 (reprint, Grand Rapids: Eerdmans, 1977), 408.

It is interesting what the king said in his decree, as recorded in verse 8. He said, "Let men call on God earnestly that each may turn from his wicked way and from the violence which is in his hands." It was not enough to have just the outward signs of repentance. He wanted genuine repentance as seen by the people's turning from their wicked ways, specifically from their violence. Nineveh and the Assyrians were primarily known for their brutality and their violence. The king was saying that they needed to turn from the very thing that characterized them.

The king then said, "Who knows, God may turn and relent and withdraw his burning anger so that we shall not perish." For a heathen king, this ruler had pretty good theology. He understood that God was under no obligation to be merciful to them. God would be perfectly just in wiping them out. The Assyrian king did not presume that God was obligated to show them mercy, and he did not demand it (as if anyone can demand something of God).

This response on the part of the people and the king—not the great storm at sea, not the great fish swallowing Jonah, not God's preserving Jonah inside the fish—is the greatest miracle in the book of Jonah. A great multitude of people in these cities repented almost immediately upon hearing God's message proclaimed.

Was this true repentance, or was it merely a desperate attempt to save themselves? We have already noted in verse 5 that the word Jonah used indicated trust in God. Jesus said something else in Matthew 12:41 that might have some bearing on this question. He said, "The men of Nineveh will stand up with this generation at the judgment, and will condemn it because they repented at the preaching of Jonah; and behold, something greater than Jonah is here." Jesus said the Ninevites repented and that they are going to stand up in the judgment and condemn the cities of Galilee that did not repent when they had the greater light of revelation in the person of Christ. Clearly this suggests that the Ninevites' repentance was indeed genuine. As incredible as it may seem, it appears that these people genuinely were converted through Jonah's preaching.[10]

There are a number of interesting parallels between Jonah and Jesus as noted in the chart below. But Jonah's mind was far-removed from the mind of Christ. Astonishingly, however, this self-centered, belligerent prophet in a single day saw a thousand times more converts than Jesus saw in his entire earthly ministry! The ways of God truly are beyond our understanding!

10. See William Hendriksen's helpful discussion in his *The Gospel of Matthew: New Testament Commentary* (Grand Rapids: Baker, 1973), 536.

JONAH AND JESUS

Jonah	**Jesus**
From Gath-hepher in Galilee (2 Kings 14:25)	From Nazareth in Galilee (Matthew 2:23)
Three days and three nights in the fish (Jonah 1:17)	Three days and three nights in the tomb (Matthew 12:40)
Ministered for three days (Jonah 3:3)	Ministered for three years
120,000 converts (Jonah 4:11)	120 converts (Acts 1:15)

We do not have much historical information from the Assyrian kingdom in the years succeeding Jonah, but we do know this. For the next fifteen years there was virtually no military activity on the part of the Assyrians.[11] Why? No doubt it was because they had repented of their violent ways in one of the most amazing miracles in all of Scripture.

GOD'S MERCY

> When God saw their deeds, that they turned from their wicked way, then God relented concerning the calamity which He had declared He would bring upon them. And He did not do it. (Jonah 3:10)

There is a third thing we see in every great spiritual awakening, and that is the mercy of God. Without the mercy of God, there is no repentance, and there is no forgiveness. Verse 10 says that God looked down and saw their deeds. Actually God knew their *hearts*, but the emphasis here is upon their *deeds*. He looked upon their deeds and saw that they humbled themselves before him, and he "relented." That is, he withheld the promised judgment. The KJV translates this "repented." That is an acceptable translation as long as we understand that this was not repentance in the sense that we usually think of it—changing from a bad course of action to a good one. God was not repenting in that sense.[12] He was withholding the judgment he had promised.

11. Georges Roux, *Ancient Iraq* (New York: Pelican, 1964), 274.

12. Marvin R. Wilson ("*naham*," *TWOT*, 2:571) says, "When *naham* is used of God, . . . the expression is anthropopathic and there is not ultimate tension. From man's limited, earthly, finite perspective it only appears that God's purposes have changed."

God did not change his mind. He did not change his purpose. From our limited human perspective, it might seem so, but again, it seems clear that Jonah preached a message to the Ninevites that was conditional. We have only a summary of that message. He said that in forty days this city was going to be destroyed, but apparently he also taught them something about who God is and what God is like. Indeed, how can one believe or trust in someone he does not know about? It seems Jonah also told them something about repentance and offered them the opportunity to repent. This would be consistent with what the Lord annunciated in Jeremiah 18:8: "If that nation against which I have spoken turns from its evil, I will relent concerning the calamity I planned to bring on it." God simply changed his announced actions in response to the change in the people of Nineveh. God was not changing his mind about anything; he was simply being true to his own nature and his own message.[13]

If there is to be a spiritual awakening in our country or anywhere else, there must be these three elements: the obedience of God's people, the repentance of unbelievers, and the mercy of God. We can control only one of those. We do not make God merciful, and we cannot make people repent. All we can do is be obedient to what God has called us to do.

There is some encouragement for us in this. God used Jonah. In fact, God made Jonah one of the greatest evangelists in history. And look at who Jonah was. God used him simply because he obeyed. Reluctantly, belatedly, he obeyed, but he did obey, and God accomplished an amazing thing through him. This tells us that God does not require that we be super-spiritual. He does not require that we know everything. He does not require a great deal of us at all, just that we obey what he has told us to do and what we know we should do and that we be willing to be used by God. That is pretty simple. We do not have to be anyone special in order to do that. And when we do it, we can be fully satisfied with whatever results God brings, whether they are large or small.

There is one rather sad postscript to this whole story. Yes, God withheld his judgment, and the people of Nineveh were not destroyed in forty days. But a hundred years later they were destroyed. According to the book of Nahum, they were destroyed for the very wickedness and violence that had characterized the Assyrians of Jonah's day (cf. Nah. 3). So within a

13. See Rolland McCune's excellent explanation of God's apparent "change" here in light of his immutability (*A Systematic Theology of Biblical Christianity*, vol. 1 [Allen Park, MI: Detroit Baptist Theological Seminary, 2009], 239–42).

hundred years of their repentance, the Assyrians had returned to their violent ways. Faith is not automatically passed on to the next generation. We see this truth very clearly in the kings of Judah. There were twenty kings in Judah's history. Only eight of those kings were godly men. Yet, if those eight godly kings also had been godly fathers, it would have had a profound effect upon Judah's history. Indeed, if they had faithfully passed on their faith to the next generation, it would have changed the course of world history.

Is there another Great Awakening coming? We do not know. That is in God's hands. God calls us, however, to be faithful in passing on our faith to our children and, as we have opportunity, to our community and our world.

PERSONAL APPLICATION

- Is there hope for a great spiritual awakening in your country? What will it take? What specifically can you do personally to help bring it about?

- What commands of God do you find most difficult to obey? Why? Write down two or three reasons you are sometimes reluctant to obey God. Outline a personal plan for successfully dealing with each of these temptations.

- What steps can you take to pass on your Christian faith to future generations?

- What does this chapter tell you about God? How should this affect your attitudes and actions?

FOR FURTHER STUDY

- Find other places in the Bible where sackcloth and ashes are mentioned. Note the occasions for employing these symbols and what they probably symbolized.

- Read some biographical sketches of several people who were influential in spiritual awakenings or of several well-known evangelists, and note some of the common characteristics of these men. Here are some suggestions: Jonathan Edwards, George Whitefield, John Wesley, Theodore Freylinghuysen, Dwight Moody, and Billy Graham. Encyclopedias such as *World Book* will include entries on most of these people. *Eerdmans Handbook to the History of Christianity*, and *Nelson's New Christian Dictionary* are also useful resources.

10

The Education of a Prophet

Jonah 4

I TEND TO BE very skeptical of fantastic claims and stories. So when I was at the grocery store and saw the headline on the tabloid that announced that the severed head of John the Baptist had been discovered, I had my doubts, to put it mildly. Needless to say, I did not spend any money to read the rest of the story.

Some fantastic claims and unbelievable stories, however, do have the ring of truth to them. Certainly the book of Jonah is a fantastic story; but while we know it is true because it is inscripturated in God's holy Word, it also has the unmistakable ring of truth to it. There is something about it that declares this *must* be true. That *something* is chapter 4. If someone had simply dreamed up the Jonah story, he or she certainly never would have written chapter 4. It just does not fit our idea of a tight, well-conceived story with a satisfying ending. It is utterly anticlimactic. This is not the way the hero of a story should act. In fact, this final chapter presents almost an absurd picture. Who can imagine an evangelist holding a great evangelistic campaign, seeing 100,000 people converted the first day, and being angry about it? The only reason this chapter is here is because it is true. Why else would it be written?

This is Jonah. He is the evangelist, angered over the stupendous results of his evangelistic campaign! Even after this great spiritual miracle, he does not have the right attitude. He still needs to be educated—or re-educated. That is what chapter 4 is about—the education of God's prophet. He has done the right things outwardly, but God must now deal with what

99

is inside Jonah. As we look at this chapter, we are going to look at the various elements of Jonah's education.

HONEST ACKNOWLEDGMENT

The first element of Jonah's education is an honest acknowledgment of what he feels. We can find many negative things to say about Jonah, and we will find still more. But at least we can say this: he was honest with God. He did not play games; he did not say what he thought God wanted to hear. He told God straight out what he thought of this whole situation. At least he was honest, and it was that honesty that opened the door for God to teach him.

His Anger

But it greatly displeased Jonah and he became angry. (Jonah 4:1)

With what was Jonah displeased? He was displeased that Nineveh was still standing—that God had spared the city. The people of Nineveh had repented, and God had withheld his judgment. Consequently, Jonah was "greatly displeased." Actually, to literally translate this from Hebrew, it would say something like this: "It was evil to Jonah, a great evil."[1] This conveys the intensity of his anger. This was not merely an annoyance to him; he was extremely angry about it. The interesting thing is that when God saw the repentance of the Ninevites, he turned *away* from his anger. Jonah turned *to* anger. This reminds us of how very different our view of things sometimes is from God's view of things. Note how this sinful attitude of Jonah twists his perception as well as his prayer.

His Prayer

He prayed to the Lord and said, "Please Lord, was not this what I said while I was still in my own country? Therefore in order to forestall this I fled to Tarshish, for I knew that You are a gracious and compassionate God, slow to anger and abundant in loving-kindness, and one who relents concerning calamity. Therefore now, O Lord, please take my life from me, for death is better to me than life." (Jonah 4:2–3)

1. Stuart says the clause expresses "Jonah's dissatisfaction about as strongly as would be possible to say it in Hebrew" (Douglas Stuart, *Hosea–Jonah.* Word Biblical Commentary, Vol, 31 [Dallas: Word, 1987], 502).

As we move into verses 2–3, we see Jonah pray. It is perhaps the strangest prayer in all the Bible. We saw Jonah pray once before in chapter 2, but there is a great contrast between that prayer and this one. His prayer in chapter 2 was a prayer of thanksgiving. It was focused upon God and what God did. This prayer is a prayer of complaint, and although it is addressed to God, the focus is upon Jonah himself. He says to the Lord, "Was not this what I said while I was still in my own country?" For the first time in the book, Jonah explains why he ran away to begin with. It was not that he was afraid to go to Nineveh, though he might have had good reason to be afraid. The thing that he really feared was that the Ninevites would be converted, and he wanted to prevent this. He wanted to see the wicked Assyrians destroyed. He hated them, and it is easy to understand why he hated them. Jonah did not want to go to Nineveh because he knew God's character.

Look at what Jonah says: "I knew that You are a gracious and compassionate God, slow to anger and abundant in lovingkindness, and one who relents concerning calamity." This is an intriguing description of God from the lips of Jonah. He acknowledged that God is "gracious." The Hebrew word is sometimes translated "pity." But it is an action word. It describes an act, not a feeling.[2] It describes a "heartfelt response by someone who has something to give to one who has a need."[3] In relation to God, it describes him as having what someone needs and giving it to that person. It is almost always used in the Old Testament of a superior responding to an inferior, whether of master to a servant or, as it is most often, of God to a man. God has something that man needs, and he gives it to him. That is what grace is.

Jonah also describes God as a "compassionate" God. "Compassion" is the feeling that accompanies the act of grace. God is gracious; he gives people what they do not have and do not deserve. This is not just a token act, however; it comes out of God's compassion, his intense feeling for that person.[4]

God is also "slow to anger." He is very patient with people. And he is "abundant in lovingkindness." This word is difficult to translate with a single word. It does speak of love, but it speaks of more than just love. It

---

2. Robert B. Girdlestone, *Synonyms of the Old Testament* (reprint, Grand Rapids: Eerdmans, 1976), 107.

3. Edwin Yamauchi, *"hanan," TWOT*, 1:302.

4. Girdlestone, *Synonyms*, 107; Leonard J. Coppes, *"raham," TWOT*, 2:841.

also speaks of faithfulness, or loyalty.[5] God is abundant in loving-kindness; he loves us faithfully, loyally. His love does not quit.

Then Jonah says God is one who "relents concerning calamity." He is desirous of withholding punishment; and when he sees repentance or change in us, he withdraws threatened punishment or judgment.

The thing to notice about this is that Jonah's description of God is completely accurate. In fact, these words come almost word for word from God's own revelation of his attributes in Exodus 34:6–7. Jonah gives a perfectly accurate description of what God is like. Clearly, Jonah knew God, but he did not share God's love and compassion and graciousness. Jonah himself had benefited from those attributes of God, just as we have, but he did not exhibit those attributes in his own life. He did not share God's love and compassion for sinners. In fact, Jonah saw God's attributes as undesirable.

We need to be very careful. If we ever become dissatisfied with who God is and what God is like, there is tremendous temptation to start to mold God into what we want him to be. And that is disastrous.

Jonah knew God. He just did not share God's attributes. He did not possess them himself. He looked at God, and said, "You are a God who relents of calamity, as I saw in Nineveh; but I don't like it. I don't like the fact that you were gracious and loving toward those people." Jonah was consumed with hatred and a desire for vengeance. But this is not God's way (cf. Deut. 32:35; Rom. 12:19–21).

How can somebody acknowledge God as loving, compassionate, gracious, and patient and not exhibit those qualities in his own life? Maybe we should ask ourselves that question, for to some degree or another, we all have been guilty of that very thing. We know God; we have been taught about him; we acknowledge him for who he is; but too often we do not see those qualities or attributes of God exhibited in our own lives. This should serve as a warning to us. We can be like Jonah—absolutely doctrinally correct, knowing the right answers and even doing the right things on the outside—and be utterly ungodly in our attitudes. It is very easy to judge ourselves as being spiritual because we know the right answers, speak the right words, teach the right doctrines, and even do the right things. But like the Pharisees, we can be inwardly rotten. Jesus described them as "whitewashed tombs" (Matt. 23:27)—they were very attractive on the outside, but inside there was only death and decay.

5. R. Laird Harris, "*hesed*," *TWOT*, 1:305; Girdlestone, *Synonyms,*113.

Jonah did the right thing. It took a while, but he obeyed God. He went to Nineveh and preached the Lord's message. But inside his attitude was corrupt. Undoubtedly, Jonah would have loved to have gone back to Israel and said, "Guess what. Nineveh has been wiped out!" He probably would have been hailed as a hero, and maybe he was looking forward to that. But instead, he could only go back and say that Nineveh had been preserved *because of his preaching*. Interestingly enough, Israel's enemy had been preserved so that they—Assyria—could one day destroy Israel, and it is possible that Jonah, like Hosea (cf. Hos. 11:5–6), may even have known that!

What all this boils down to is that Jonah was very worldly-minded. He was thinking only of himself. In fact, we see this in verse 3. He said to the Lord, "Please take my life from me, for death is better to me than life." At this point Jonah was healthy, but he preferred death to living without getting what he wanted. He was totally selfish.[6]

There is another facet of Jonah we should not overlook here. For all his faults, we must say that Jonah did have faith. He had enough faith to believe that God could and would bring about the conversion of the pagan inhabitants of Nineveh! We may not consider ourselves as rebellious as Jonah, and certainly he is not one to emulate in most respects. But do we have the faith this rebellious prophet evidenced? Do we pray, believing God can do the impossible?

DIVINE REBUKE

It was time for God to speak and to initiate the second and most crucial part of Jonah's education. God's words took the form of a rebuke.

God's Question

The Lord said, "Do you have good reason to be angry?"
(Jonah 4:4)

When God asked Jonah if he had good reason to be angry, the answer to that question was clear, but Jonah did not respond.[7] God then proceeded to give to Jonah an object lesson.

---

6. It is fair to say that most—though not all—people who commit or contemplate suicide (self-murder) are, like Jonah, utterly selfish. It may, in fact, be the ultimate act of selfishness.

7. See David J. Clark, Norm Mundhenk, Eugene A. Nida, and Brynmor F. Price (*A*

God's Object Lesson

> Then Jonah went out from the city and sat east of it. There he made
> a shelter for himself and sat under it in the shade until he could see
> what would happen in the city. So the Lord God appointed a plant
> and it grew up over Jonah to be a shade over his head to deliver
> him from his discomfort. And Jonah was extremely happy about
> the plant. But God appointed a worm when dawn came the next
> day and it attacked the plant and it withered. When the sun came
> up God appointed a scorching east wind, and the sun beat down
> on Jonah's head so that he became faint and begged with all his
> soul to die, saying, "Death is better to me than life." (Jonah 4:5–8)

Jonah went to a place east of the city and camped out there. There he con-
structed a shelter to protect himself from the scorching heat of the day,
and he "sat under it in the shade until he could see what would happen in
the city." What was he hoping to see? We are not told. He may have been
hoping that God would change his mind and destroy this city. Perhaps
he was thinking that this was a shallow repentance that would last only a
short time, and then God would have to destroy the city. Maybe, however,
he was waiting, hoping that God would do something that would explain
all this to him.

We must understand from the verses that follow that the shelter
Jonah built was probably made of leaves, something that withered rather
quickly in the heat, because when we come to verse 6 he is apparently
without shelter from the heat of the sun. While he continued to sit there,
however, "the Lord God appointed a plant and it grew up over Jonah," giving him shade and relief "from his discomfort."[8] Apparently, the first shelter withered; so God caused this plant to grow up over Jonah to give him
shade. We know from verse 10 that it grew up overnight. Jonah was sitting
in the heat of the sun, and God actually performed a miracle in order to
give him some shade. Understandably, Jonah was "extremely happy" about
this shade that God had provided.

Note how quickly Jonah's mood changes, however. He had only
one full day to enjoy the shade of this plant, for verse 7 tells us, "God appointed a worm when dawn came the next day and it attacked the plant

---

Handbook on the Books of Obadiah, Jonah, and Micah [New York: United Bible Societies,
1993], 106–7) for a discussion of the translation of verse 4.

8. "Appointed" in Jonah 4:6, 7, and 8 is a translation of the same Hebrew word used
in 1:17. See *BDB*, 584.

and it withered." God miraculously gave Jonah shade, but only for one day. God then took the shade away by sending a worm to kill the plant. Jonah's situation now is even worse than it had been before. He is sitting in the heat. And when the sun came up, God sent a "scorching east wind" that together with the sun beating down on Jonah created an unbearable situation for the prophet. He "became faint" and again pleaded with God to take his life, saying, "Death is better to me than life."

Remember this is Mesopotamia, or present-day Iraq. During the hot season in Mesopotamia, the mean maximum temperature is 110 degrees F.[9] But God sent a "scorching east wind" upon him. This superheated wind is known as a sirocco. It can raise the temperature another 15 to 20 degrees in a few hours.[10] Jonah now was extremely uncomfortable, even miserable. Can one survive such conditions? Of course one can survive as long as he does not dehydrate. But Jonah begged for death. He was pouting, he was selfish, he was self-absorbed, and now he was physically miserable.

It is interesting to note that people who are self-absorbed find it very difficult to endure any real pain or misery. They are focused totally on themselves, and with the least little pain or difficulty, they are ready to give up. They are ready even to die. Jonah was uncomfortable to be sure, but his death wish was as much the result of his self-centeredness as it was his discomfort.

All of this was an object lesson for Jonah. God had caused this plant to grow up miraculously in order to deliver Jonah from the discomfort of the oppressive heat. And this made Jonah extremely happy. What was God telling him? Jonah rejoiced over his deliverance from his discomfort, but he did not rejoice over the deliverance of Nineveh from destruction. He rejoiced over a little shade from the sun, but there was no rejoicing when people were converted and saved from destruction. Similarly, Jonah became distressed over the death of this plant, but he was not a bit distressed at the possibility of the Assyrians in Nineveh being destroyed. In fact, he was anxious for it to happen. God was showing Jonah his wicked, misplaced priorities and the shallowness of his faith. Jonah possessed nothing of God's grace and compassion and love for these people.

9. H. L. Ellison, "Jonah" in *Expositor's Bible Commentary*, ed. Frank E. Gaebelein, Vol. 7 (Grand Rapids: Zondervan, 1985), 387.

10. Alfred H. Joy, "wind" in *International Standard Bible Encyclopaedia*, ed. James Orr (Grand Rapids: Eerdmans, 1939), 3086.

God's Second Question

> Then God said to Jonah, "Do you have good reason to be angry about the plant?" And he said, "I have good reason to be angry, even to death." (Jonah 4:9)

God goes on to offer his final word, which reinforces this whole object lesson. God again asks Jonah if he has good reason to be angry, this time asking specifically about his anger over the plant. Jonah answers God's question this time, saying, "I have good reason to be angry, even to death." These are the last recorded words of Jonah. God's actions made no sense to him. He claims he has good reason to be angry. Yet the fact that Jonah wrote this book is an admission on the part of the prophet that he was a very selfish, worldly-minded, materialistic person. And God's actions never make sense to such self-centered people.

God's Lesson

> Then the Lord said, "You had compassion on the plant for which you did not work and which you did not cause to grow, which came up overnight and perished overnight. Should I not have compassion on Nineveh, the great city in which there are more than 120,000 persons who do not know the difference between their right and left hand, as well as many animals?" (Jonah 4:10–11)

God was not the one who was inconsistent in his thinking and his actions. It was Jonah. Jonah had compassion for a single plant he did not plant or cultivate, and he was greatly troubled by the plant's destruction; yet he was angered when God showed compassion on Nineveh, a city of "more than 120,000 persons." The reference to 120,000 persons who did not "know the difference between their right and left hand" is taken by many to refer to children. However, the Hebrew word "persons" (*adam*) is never used in the Old Testament for children.[11] The Lord seems to be describing the total number of people who were converted. This description of them is not to be taken literally—that they did not know right from left. It is meant to describe people who lack spiritual, moral perception. In other words, they were lost. They did not have any concept of what is truly moral and right, yet these 120,000 people were converted at Jonah's preaching. This was undoubtedly the greater part of the population of Greater Nineveh.

11. *Adam* is normally used for mankind in general or as the personal name of the first man. See Leonard J. Coppes, "*adam*," *TWOT*, 1:10 and *BDB*, 9.

God is saying, "Jonah, you were concerned about a single plant that you had nothing to do with. You did not plant it or cultivate it. Should I not be concerned about 120,000 people whom I created—people who are made in my image?" What a rebuke this was to God's prophet.

The Lord then added an interesting, almost mysterious, phrase at the end about his compassion not only on the people of Nineveh but also on the animals. Why are the animals mentioned? It is not altogether clear why this expression is used here, but I tend to agree with Desmond Alexander that God was in a sense being sarcastic. He was saying that if Jonah was not concerned about 120,000 people, maybe he at least would be moved by the thought of their animals being destroyed along with them.[12] After all, he was concerned about a plant!

There was no response from Jonah. We assume he continued with this wrong attitude, at least for the time being. We know that eventually it changed because Jonah wrote this book, describing himself in very unflattering terms. We can safely assume that he did repent of his hateful attitude, but at this point there was no response, only God's rebuke.

Jonah's problem at this point was not intellectual. He could have passed the theology exam. He knew what God is like. He knew God. Jonah's problem was moral. Although he knew God, he did not share God's viewpoint. He did not share God's love and compassion for people. Jonah also knew Scripture. In fact, as we saw in chapter 2, he knew Scripture thoroughly; but he was absorbed with himself. He loved himself more than he loved God, and that was the whole problem.

Peter was another of God's servants who failed him. But after Peter's failure, Jesus came to him and said, "Do you love Me? . . . Do you love Me? . . . Do you love Me?" (John 21:15, 16, 17). He did not say, "Peter, you have sinned greatly, and you need to change." Peter knew that. Jesus said, "Do you love Me?" We may sometimes be like Jonah or Peter. We may be capable Bible students, but do we love him? We may be outwardly faithful in our duties and our service, but do we love him? Do we love him for who he is, for what he does, and for what he has done? Do we love him? That was the question Jonah needed to answer. It was the question Peter needed to answer. It is the question we need to answer—every day.

---

12. Desmond Alexander, "Jonah" in David W. Baker, T. Desmond Alexander, and Bruce K. Waltke, *Obadiah, Jonah and Micah* (Downer's Grove, IL: InterVarsity, 1988), 130–31.

Personal Application

- Are you open and honest in your relationship with God? Why or why not?

- Do you possess any of the negative attitudes of Jonah? How are these manifested in your life? What is the key to ridding yourself of them?

- Can you look back to a time in your life when your priorities were misplaced? What caused this? What can you do to make sure this does not happen again?

- How do you respond to sincere rebuke? Read the following verses in the book of Proverbs, and commit at least one verse to memory: 3:11–12; 12:1, 15; 28:23.

- Try to honestly evaluate your love for God. Are there things or people you love more than God? What is the true measure of your love for God? Try to answer this last question before looking up the following verses and meditating on them: John 14:15–21; 1 John 2:15–17; 3:11–18.

For Further Study

- Use a Bible atlas or Bible encyclopedia or a general encyclopedia (remember to look under "Iraq") to learn about the topography and climate of Nineveh and its environs.

- Peruse some newspapers or news magazines for contemporary examples of those who value animals or things above human beings. How can this be explained from a biblical perspective?

- Watch *Jonah: A VeggieTales Movie* on videocassette or DVD. Does it portray the message of Jonah accurately, even though it takes obvious liberties with the historical record? Is such a humorous approach a useful teaching tool?

Bibliography

Achtemeier, Elizabeth. *Minor Prophets I*. New International Biblical Commentary. Peabody, MA: Hendrickson, 1996.

Alexander, Desmond. "Jonah" in David W. Baker, T. Desmond Alexander, and Bruce K. Waltke, *Obadiah, Jonah and Micah*. Downer's Grove, IL.: InterVarsity, 1988.

Allen, Leslie C. *The Books of Obadiah, Jonah and Micah*. New International Commentary on the Old Testament. Grand Rapids: Eerdmans, 1976.

Amerding, Carl. "Obadiah" in *Expositor's Bible Commentary*. Vol. 7, Frank Gaebelein, ed. Grand Rapids: Zondervan, 1985.

Archer, Gleason. *A Survey of Old Testament Introduction*. Chicago: Moody, 1974.

Baker, David W. "Obadiah" in David W. Baker, T. Desmond Alexander, and Bruce K. Waltke, *Obadiah, Jonah and Micah*. Downer's Grove, IL.: InterVarsity, 1988.

Baker, Walter L. "Obadiah" in *The Bible Knowledge Commentary*. Vol. 1, John F. Walvoord and Roy B. Zuck, eds. Wheaton, IL.: Victor Books, 1985.

Baldwin, Joyce. "Jonah" in *The Minor Prophets: An Exegetical and Expository Commentary*. Vol. 2. Thomas Edward McComisky, ed. Grand Rapids: Baker, 1993.

Beyer, Bryan, and John Walton. *Bible Study Commentary: Obadiah, Jonah*. Grand Rapids: Zondervan, 1988.

Boice, James Montgomery. *The Minor Prophets*. Grand Rapids: Zondervan, 1983.

Bromiley, Geoffrey, ed. *The International Standard Bible Encyclopedia*. Rev. Grand Rapids: Eerdmans, 1979.

Brown, Francis; S. R. Driver; and C. A. Briggs. *A Hebrew and English Lexicon of the Old Testament*. Reprint, Oxford: Clarendon. 1978.

Clark, David J.; Norm Mundhenk; Eugene A Nida; and Brynmor F. Price. *A Handbook on the Books of Obadiah, Jonah, and Micah*. New York: United Bible Societies, 1993.

DeVries, LaMoine F. *Cities of the Biblical World*. Peabody, MA: Hendrickson, 1997.

Dillard, Raymond B., and Tremper Longman III. *An Introduction to the Old Testament*. Grand Rapids: Zondervan, 1994.

Douglas, J. D., ed. *The New Bible Dictionary*. Grand Rapids: Eerdmans, 1962.

Ellison, H. L. "Jonah" in *Expositor's Bible Commentary*. Vol. 7, Frank E. Gaebelein, ed., Grand Rapids: Zondervan, 1985.

Elwell, Walter A., ed. *The Evangelical Dictionary of Theology*. 2d ed., Grand Rapids: Baker Academic, 2001.

Feinberg, Charles L. *The Minor Prophets*. Chicago: Moody, 1990.

Fink, Paul R. "Obadiah" and "Jonah" in *Liberty Bible Commentary*. Jerry Falwell, Edward Hindson, and Woodrow Kroll, eds. Nashville: Thomas Nelson, 1982.

Freeman, Hobart E. *An Introduction to the Old Testament Prophets*. Chicago: Moody, 1968.

Gasque, W. Ward. "Obadiah" in *The International Bible Commentary with the New International Version*. F. F. Bruce, gen. ed. Grand Rapids: Zondervan, 1986.

Girdlestone, Robert B. *Synonyms of the Old Testament*. Reprint, Grand Rapids: Eerdmans, 1976.

Griffiths, Michael C. "Jonah" in *The International Bible Commentary with the New International Version*. F. F. Bruce, gen. ed. Grand Rapids: Zondervan, 1986.

Harris, R. Laird; Gleason L Archer; and Bruce K Waltke, eds. *Theological Wordbook of the Old Testament*. 2 Vols, Chicago: Moody, 1980.

Hellerman, Joe. "A Commentary on the Book of Obadiah." Th.M. Thesis. Talbot School of Theology, 1987.

Hill, Andrew E., and John H. Walton. *A Survey of the Old Testament*. Grand Rapids: Zondervan, 2000.

Jamieson, Robert; A. R Fausset; and David Brown. *A Commentary Critical, Experimental, and Practical on the Old and New Testaments*. 3 Vols. Grand Rapids: Eerdmans, n.d.

Keil, C. F. and Franz Delitzsch. *Commentary on the Old Testament*, Vol. 10. Reprint, Grand Rapids: Eerdmans, 1977.

Kitchen, K. A. *The Bible in Its World*. Downer's Grove, IL: InterVarsity, 1978.

Kittel, Rudolph. *Biblia Hebraica Stuttgartensia*. Stuttgart, Germany: Deutsche Biblelstiftung, 1967/77.

Laetsch, Theo. *Bible Commentary: The Minor Prophets*. St. Louis: Concordia, 1956.

Livingston, G. Herbert. "Jonah" in *The Wycliffe Bible Commentary*, ed. Charles F Pfeiffer and Everett F Harrison.. Chicago: Moody, 1962.

Mayhue, Richard L. "The Prophet's Watchword: Day of the Lord." *Grace Theological Journal*. Vol. 6, no. 2. (1985): 231–46.

Merrill, Eugene. *An Historical Survey of the Old Testament*. Nutley, NJ: Craig, 1966.

Morgan, G. Campbell. *The Minor Prophets: The Men and Their Messages*. Westwood, NJ: Revell, 1960.

Niehaus, Jeffrey J. "Obadiah" in *The Minor Prophets: An Exegetical and Expository Commentary*. Vol. 2. Thomas Edward McComiskey, ed. Grand Rapids: Baker, 1993.

Ogilvie, Lloyd J. *The Communicator's Commentary: Hosea, Joel, Amos, Obadiah, Jonah*. Waco: Word, 1991.

Orr, James, ed. *The International Standard Bible Encyclopaedia*. 4 vols. Reprint, Grand Rapids: Eerdmans, 1980.

Owens, John Joseph. *Analytical Key to the Old Testament*. 4 vols. Grand Rapids: Baker, 1989.

Pfeiffer, Charles F. *An Outline of Old Testament History*. Chicago: Moody, 1960.

Pritchard, James B., ed. *The Ancient Near East: An Anthology of Texts and Pictures*, vol. 1. Princeton: Princeton University Press, 1958.

Pusey, E. B. *The Minor Prophets—A Commentary*. Grand Rapids: Baker, 1950.

Roux, Georges. *Ancient Iraq*. New York: Penguin, 1964.

Stuart, Douglas. *Hosea–Jonah*. Word Biblical Commentary. Vol. 31. Dallas: Word, 1987.

Thompson, J. A. *The Bible and Archaeology*. Grand Rapids: Eerdmans, 1962.

Twombly, Gerald H. *Major Themes from the Minor Prophets*. Winona Lake, IN.: BMH Books, 1981.

Watts, John D. W. *Obadiah: A Critical Exegetical Commentary*. Grand Rapids: Eerdmans, 1969.

Whitcomb, John C. Notes accompanying the audiotape series "The Book of Jonah," Hagerstown: MD: Whitcomb Ministries, n.d.

Williams, Ronald J. *Hebrew Syntax: An Outline*. 2nd ed. Toronto: University of Toronto Press, 1976.

Wood, Leon J. *A Survey of Israel's History*. Grand Rapids: Zondervan, 1970.

www.ingramcontent.com/pod-product-compliance
Lightning Source LLC
Chambersburg PA
CBHW070500090426
42735CB00012B/2634